CORGI CLASSICS
Price Guide
1st Edition

Publisher & Editor: Simon Epton

Copyright © Toy Price Guide

ISBN 978-0-9565015-5-4

Designed in the UK by KK Design Services

Printed in the UK by Buxton Press

Published in the UK by the Toy Price Guide

Pictures by the author unless stated

Advertising; Tel 01205 820792 or mob. 07403 858728

Email: info@toypriceguide.co.uk

Front cover images:
31010 Short Bros. Scammell Highwayman Low Loader with Luffing Shovel
47204 Avro York RAF Kings Flight (Aviation Archive)
97057 Leyland PSI & Leyland Leopard OOC set
US55031 PCC Streetcar South Eastern Pennsylvania Transport Authority

Registered Address:
Toy Price Guide, 7 Sherbourne Close, Swineshead, Boston, Lincs PE20 3LE
Tel 01205 820792 or 07403 858728

Contents

Our guide lists nearly 5500 models released after Mattel went into receivership in 1983 to the 2008 purchase by Hornby. For individual model identification use the detailed contents listing below to locate the page number your model appears, which should be listed both by type and by catalogue number. Gift sets can be found at the end of each section

SPECIAL THANKS

The Toy Price Guide is committed to working with quality toy specialists whose services we recommend to collectors; in particular we would like to thank the following advertisers for their support; Richardsons, Warwick & Warwick & DJ Auctions. Special thanks also to the following collectors; Pete Stephenson, David Storey and Peter Hurst for their help in compiling the listings contained within this publication.

ADVERTISING INDEX

CONTACT US

Editor & Publisher - Simon Epton info@toypriceguide.co.uk

To become a Trade Stockist email us on info@toypriceguide.co.uk

MacFarlane MAN TGA Curtainside & Bassett Scania Curtainside. Sold for £60 DJ Actions

Mercedes Actros Curtainside pair; Knauf & Curran. Sold for £45 DJ Auctions

Fridge Trailers pair; Payne Volvo & Thomas Gibb Scania. Sold for £55 DJ Auctions

Step Frame Trailers pair; DAF XF & Alpha Nooteboom. Sold for £95 DJ Auctions

Wrekin Roadways set. Sold for £45 DJ Auctions

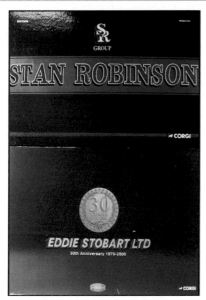

Pair; Stan Robinson & Eddie Stobart
30th Anniversary sets.
Sold for £90 DJ Auctions

Pair; Gibb's & Pollock sets.
Sold for £95 DJ Auctions

Pair; Eddie Stobart Story & Scania @ Stobart sets.
Sold for £65 DJ Auctions

Pair; Benton Bros & Alan Lodge sets.
Sold for £90 DJ Auctions

EDITORS WELCOME

Thank you to everyone who purchased our earlier Corgi Toys Price Guide listing the vintage models produced before the company went into receivership in 1983. The Corgi Classic Price Guide is the natural follow on and includes models were the last guide finished through to those produced prior to the company being purchased by Hornby. Once again we have teamed up with leading collecting experts and specialist UK toy auction houses to bring you this price guide.

Our guide is the **ONLY** current price guide dedicated to Corgi Classic models and has been compiled using our archive of original catalogues, conversations with dealers, access to private collections, several decades spent gathering content at collector's fairs, traditional auction salerooms and more recently online auctions, plus the assistance of Mike Forbes former editor of Diecast Collector magazine and my experience as Publisher of both Diecast Collector & Collectors Gazette publications.

Where possible 'real prices' have been used for individual items sold in 2011 and postage where items are sold via the internet. Items sold at UK auction houses exclude commission. As prices vary we recommend allowing a 10% margin of error as well as taking into consideration the auctioneer's commission (generally 10-15%).

We are always looking out for fresh information, errors or omissions so if spot any item in your collection missing from our guide please make us aware and we will include it in a later edition, which we hope to bring out to include the models subsequently issued by Hornby. Details of how to contact us appear on page 3 or you can get in touch via our website using the 'contact us' page.

Happy Collecting!
Simon Epton

ABOUT THE TOY PRICE GUIDE

Simon Epton was born in Lincolnshire and worked in the Publishing industry for many years during which time he launched Diecast Collector, TV Film Memorabilia and also published Collectors Gazette, Collect it! and the Ramsay Price Guides.
Simon regularly writes articles for national magazines and provides toy expert advice for several long running television series on antiques and collectables.
This is his 10th price guide publication and 7 others are currently available including; Action Man (£4.99), Britains Toys 2nd Edition (£9.99), Classic TV & Film Toys (£6.99), Hornby Trains (£7.99), Corgi Toys (£9.99), Tri-ang Toys (£8.99) & English & French Dinky Toys 2nd Edition (£9.99)

The Toy Price Guide is a unique publishing company with a keen interest in the history of toys and is dedicated to building a range of special interest Toy & Childhood Memorabilia publications, both in print form and online, enabling collectors or those selling collectables to identify the market value for their collection.

Pickfords Heavy Haulage Industrial set.
Sold for £60 DJ Auctions

Henor Haulage Heavy Haulage set.
Sold for £75 DJ Auctions

Eddie Stobart Scammell Contractor set.
Sold for £70 DJ Auctions

The Great Book of Corgi.
Sold for £60 Toy Price Guide Archive

4 Heavy Haulage models.
Sold for £80 DJ Auctions

A group of 4 Beatles Collection models
comprising; Yellow Submarine, Newspaper Taxi,
Magical Mystery tour Bus & Graffiti Van.
Sold for £100 DJ Auctions

THE CURRENT MARKET

Much has been spoken about the after market prices for Corgi Classics and, during my time on Diecast Collector and Collectors Gazette magazines, the editorial team certainly witnessed many such letters from collectors. Turn the clock back 50-55 years, although circumstances were very different, the same would be said of vintage Corgi models as it took several years for these to appreciate in value. My most recent observations on the value of Corgi Classics is that 5 years ago blocks of 20 models per lot were a regular occurrence at UK auction rooms, now though we are finding these blocks of models have reduced in size and in many instances only include 2-3 models achieving the same price as previously larger lots. So something is happening!

There is also a growing interest from Europe, particularly Italy and Holland, where the appetite of collectors for Corgi Toys coupled with the low value of the pound against the Euro is making it attractive for them to collect and build a collection of the Classics range.

That said collect for pleasure, not profit are our words of advice to anyone looking to build a collection, the pleasure should be in the hunt! Though it is reassuring to hear your collection is appreciating in value. Despite the well documented financial pressures still affecting peoples spending habits prices remain strong for the shorter run Limited Editions, factory errors, Heavy Haulage, several of the military range and also brewery related items. As ever condition is vitally important and we always recommend you check the box contents as most of the Classics came with a printed certificate (if it numbered as one of the first 10 even better), the correct leaflet, internal packaging and if possible still sealed in it's factory tissue paper. All these will add to the value of your model as you will be surprised how many do not contain these when they reach the after sales market.

To establish the value of a particular model/box we have produced a Price Calculator on the following page, however it is always worth remembering the value of toys, particularly those sold via auctions, is dependent on 2 buyers wanting the same item so it should be used as an estimate only.

Disclaimer

Guide prices quoted are not intended to represent the price a dealer will offer it for sale, as the dealer more often is carrying expenses to offer customers a quality and reliable collecting service, which costs money to maintain. The price guide information does not constitute, nor should it be construed as, financial advice for investment purposes and as it states should be used as a guide only. The publisher, its agents and contributors shall not be liable for any loss or damage whatsoever arising as a result of reliance on any information contained within this guide.

This publication has been compiled solely for use as a reference guide. Whilst every care has been taken in compiling the guide the publisher cannot accept any responsibility whatsoever for errors and omissions or any financial loss, which may occur, as a result of its use.

Prices correct at the time of going to press on 1st May 2010

Heavy Haulage Trio; DAF Space Cab with Tender
load, DAF Super Space Cab with loco load
& Atkinson Adventurer with Boiler load.
Sold for £170 DJ Auctions

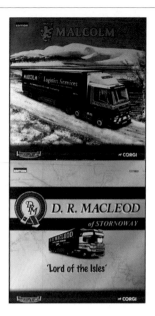

Pair; Malcolm & Macleod 'Lord of the Isles' sets.
Sold for £90 DJ Auctions

Pair; Moreton & Cullimore sets.
Sold for £75 DJ Auctions

6 bus & coach models from the Connoisseur
Collection including Leyland Royal Tiger, Bedford
Val, Burlingham Seagull & AEC Routemaster.
Sold for £40 DJ Auctions

TOY PRICE GUIDE CALCULATOR

The guide price is based on mint/nr mint boxed items sold in 2011. The value of Corgi Classics is particularly dependent on an individual items quality, packaging, presence of its unique limited edition certificate and miniature point of sale advertising and information literature that came with each item. Items with damaged/missing packaging, literature and at worst broken parts are worth only a fraction of the mint-boxed price. The scale below may help collectors apply values to their own collection:

Boxed Model Value Calculator

Mint – perfect ex-shop condition complete with literature.....................................100%

Mint – perfect ex-shop condition missing certificate/literature..........................60-80%

VG-Excellent – showing signs of minor box wear 50-60%

Unboxed – mint but missing packaging, literature, certificate, etc....................40-50%

Damaged & unboxed with broken parts .... 30% *

* Model restorers in particular seek out damaged models keeping prices higher than would be expected.

TERMS OF REFERENCE & ABBREVIATIONS

The following abbreviations have been used to describe the condition and price of toys:

MIB	Mint in original Box	**PO**	Post Office
AA	Automobile Association	**U/B**	Unboxed
Ex	Excellent condition	**VW**	Volkswagen
RAC	Royal Automobile Club	**NPA**	No price available
VG	Very good condition	**RN**	Rally/Race Number

4 James Bond Aston Martin DB5's; Collect 99,
Tomorrow Never Dies, 40th Anniversary 7
Golden Eye. Sold for £95 DJ Auctions

The Definitive Bond Collection.
Sold for £20 Toy Price Guide Archive

Thorneycroft & Guy Arab London Transport buses.
Sold for £18 Toy Price Guide Archive

Mansel Davies & Son Volvo Tanker.
Sold for £50 DJ Auctions

Corby Chilled Scania Fridge Trailer. Sold for £35 DJ Auctions

1983 - Following the demise of Mettoy, Corgi's parent company, the company was put into receivership

1984 - A management buy-out created a new company Corgi Toys Ltd on 29th March 1984. The toy range continued together with a few newly introduced models. Although concentrating on Commercial vehicles it was clear the market had moved away from children's toys to adult nostalgia collectables leading to more models of older vehicles being produced. This observation signalled the re-birth of Corgi.

1987 - The first of the classic range of 1:50 scale buses, the duple bodied Bedford, was introduced. Due to cost constraints quality control was relaxed resulting in several rare printing errors and variations emerging which are now sought after by collectors. Early yellow and blue boxes were replaced by window boxes enabling collectors to view the contents, blue for toy issues and grey for commercials.

1:43 scale was chosen for cars and vans which fitted with several other international manufacturers allowing for a mix of models to be displayed together. The success of Lledo Days Gone and Matchbox Yesteryears confirmed thoughts that the same castings could be produced in numerous liveries so small commercials were the obvious choice. The Morris Minor van arrived in 1987.

Voted British Toy Company of the Year by the National Association of Toy Retailers.

1988 - Corgi Classics introduces the Morris Minor 1000 saloon, it's first 1:43 scale car in this range quickly followed by Jaguar and several other models.

1989 – Mattel purchases Corgi Toys Ltd and renames the company Corgi Classics

1990 – Production moves to China from Swansea with the first model being the MGA in British racing green.

1991 – Swansea facility closed and administration moved to Mattel's Leicester head office. The Mini mould was revised for the first time since 1976

1994 - The company introduce the Original Omnibus Company 1:76 scale range (OOC). New tooling aimed at the American market featuring commercials, fire vehicles and coaches introduced.

1995 – Corgi Classic Ltd bought from Mattel by management buy-out led Cinven.

1996 – Corgi Classics acquires Basset Lowke (Trains). Character licenses for the Beatles and Mr Bean secured and the Hong Kong transport range introduced.

1998 – Corgi Classics introduce their Modern Trucks range differentiating them from their 'Classics' (old lorries range). Also this year the Aviation Archive line of diecast military airplanes and the ICON figure range are introduced.

1999 – Corgi Classics sold to Zindart, an American company responsible mass producing collectables from their Chinese factory, where Corgi Classics were made. It also opened the door to exclusively tooled models for the US market.

Corgi debuted the Aviation Archive line of diecast military airplanes. Beginning with 1/72 scale.

2000 – Corgi Classics Ltd acquires Lledo

A new line of 1:50 scale military vehicles from World War II introduced.

2001 – Completely new mould made for the Mini

2003 – The Dr Who range is launched, the first ever in diecast

2006 – Diecast, hand painted metal soldier figures introduced the Forward March series to compliment their 1:32 and 1:50 scale military vehicles.

2008 – Hornby acquires Corgi Classics Limited for £8.3 million

BUY OR SELL YOUR CORGI CLASSICS AT THESE GREAT TOY COLLECTORS FAIRS

~~M~~ay 2011
~~Tue~~sday   3rd   Rugby evening
~~Su~~nday   8th   Coventry
~~Su~~nday   15th   Rugby Vintage
~~Sat~~urday   21st   Sandown Park

~~Ju~~ne 2011
~~Su~~nday   5th   NEC Birmingham
~~Su~~nday   12th   Stafford Showground
~~Su~~nday   19th   Buxton

~~Jul~~y 2011
~~Su~~nday   3rd   Reebok Stadium
~~Tue~~sday   5th   Rugby evening
~~Su~~nday   10th   Coventry

~~Au~~gust 2011
~~Su~~nday   14th   Stafford Showground

~~Se~~ptember 2011
~~Sat~~urday   3rd   Sandown Park
~~Su~~nday   4th   Trafford Centre
~~Tue~~sday   6th   Rugby evening

September 2011
Sunday   11th   Buxton
Sunday   18th   Coventry
Sunday   25th   NEC Birmingham

October 2011
Saturday   1st   Rugby Vintage
Sunday   2nd   Stafford Showground
Sunday   16th   Reebok Stadium

November 2011
Tuesday   1st   Rugby evening
Sunday   13th   Buxton
Saturday   19th   Sandown Park
Sunday   20th   Kettering
Sunday   27th   Harrogate

December 2011
Sunday   4th   Trafford Centre
Sunday   11th   Stafford Showground
Tuesday   27th   NEC Birmingham
Thursday   29th   Reebok Stadium

Hundreds of Corgi models bought and sold at every fair
Find out more at www.bpfairs.com
Tel: 01604 846688 or 07966 527177

Adams ERF ECT Olympic Curtainside.
Sold for £22 DJ Auctions

Eddie Stobart pair; Mercedes Atros Fridge
Trailer & Scania Topline Curtainside.
Sold for £32 DJ Auctions

Scania Curtainside pair; Pete Osbourne Logistics &
Currieuropean. Sold for £30 DJ Auctions

Pair; Gretna FC Foden & Hannon International DAF.
Sold for £40 DJ Auctions

Gallacher's Man Curtainside. Sold for £25 DJ Auctions

Toy Collectors Auction

uctions Ltd
neers & Valuers

DJ Auctions Ltd
Auctioneers & Valuers

at Sir Stuart Goodwin Hall, The Showground, Winthorpe, Newark, Notts, NG24 2NY

HE MIDLANDS PREMIER
OY AUCTION!

LIVE BIDDING ONLINE!

**five dedicated Saturday toy sales per year held at the
cious Newark Showground, situated only 1 mile from the A1**

Corgi Heavy Haulage Pickfords Industrial Ltd Set. Mint in Excellent box. **Estimate £30 - 40, Price realised £60**

Complete Set of Corgi Chipperfields Circus Vehicles including AEC Cage Truck and Trailer, Foden Closed Pole Truck with Caravan, ERF 8 Wheel Rigid Truck, Bedford Advanced Booking Vehicles and Bedford Horse Transporter. Mint in Excellent boxes. **Estimate £100 - 130, Price realised £160**

Heavy Haulage including DAF with Loco Tender Load, DAF ace Cab with Loco Load and Adventurer with Boiler Load. lint in Excellent boxes. **£40 - 60, Price realised £170**

2 x Corgi 1:50th Scale Modern Trucks Sets including Gibbs End of the Road Fraserburgh and Scotland's Finest Pollock. Mint in Excellent boxes. **Estimate £40 - 60 Price realised £200**

98751 Chitty Chitty Bang Bang. ver, Black, Red and Orange. Mint box complete with Plinth an tificates. **Estimate £40 - 60 Price realised £45**

2 x Corgi 1:50th Scale Modern Trucks Sets including Norfolk Line and HE Payne Transport. Mint in Excellent boxes. **Estimate £30 - 50 Price realised £110**

es realised and future sales dates are available on our website:

ww.dj-auctions.co.uk

: 01642 649331   Email: info@dj-auctions.co.uk

Pair; Gretna FC Foden & Hannon International DAF.
Sold for £40 DJ Auctions

Pair; Gretna FC Foden & Hannon International DAF.
Sold for £40 DJ Auctions

Pair; G Own Scania & McMullan Volvo Curtainside.
Sold for £40 DJ Auctions

Pair; Duncan Hill Scania & Rawlings Mercedes.
Sold for £30 DJ Auctions

Feenstra Renault Fridge Trailer. Sold for £20 DJ Auctions

Corgi JCB 1/50 scale CC11914 ERF EC Nooteboom Step Frame Trailer & JS220 Excavator. Limited Edition 1357/1510. Sold for £45 Aston's.

Corgi Heavy Haulage 1/50 scale CC13242 DAF XF Super Space CAB Nooteboom Step Frame Trailer & Volvo Articulated Hauler A25D - Leicester Heavy Haulage. Limited Edition 179/1510. Sold for £45 Aston's.

Corgi Heavy Haulage CC14007 Volvo FH Nooteboom Step Frame Trailer & Volvo Excavator Wheel EW180B East West Heavy Haulage 1/50 scale. Limited edition 1268/1510. Sold for £45 Aston's.

Corgi Heavy Haulage CC13816 Mercedes-Benz Actros Nooteboom Low Loader & Volvo Excavator EC210 - JB Rawcliffe & Sons Ltd. 1/50 scale. Limited Edition 1269/1510. Sold for £45 Aston's.

Corgi Heavy Haulage CC13427 Man TGA Nooteboom Low Loader, JCB 456 Wheel Loader ZX & Vauxhall Vivaro Escort Van - R Collett & Sons (Transport) Ltd. 1/50 scale. Limited edition 1298/1510. Sold for £45 Aston's.

C864/6 Ford Model T tanker in Olympic Gasoline livery, 7500 Limited Edition issued in 1986. Sold for £7 Toy Price Guide Archive

CARS

1:18 SCALE SERIES

MGB Roadster

	Ref.	Model	Price
❑	45201	Yellow - soft top	£15
❑	95103	Red	£15
❑	95104	White	£15
❑	95106	Racing green - plinth mounted	£22

MGF

❑	46601	Amaranth	£12-16
❑	46602	Racing green	£12-16
❑	46603	Signal red	£12-16
❑	46702	Japan Racing	£12-16
❑	46703	Rover	£12-16
❑	95100	White	£12-16
❑	95101	Red	£12-16
❑	95102	Racing green	£12-16
❑	95105	Charcoal grey - plinth mounted	£24

Bentley 3L, 1927

❑	9001	Green	£30-35
❑	9002	Red	£30-35
❑	9004	Green - World of Wooster	£40-45

Daimler 38hp, 1910

❑	9021	Red	£25-30

Model T Ford, 1915

❑	9011	Black	£25-30
❑	9012	Yellow	£25-30
❑	9013	Light blue	£25-30

Renault 12/16, 1910

❑	9031	Lavender	£25-30
❑	9032	Yellow	£25-30

Rolls Royce Silver Ghost, 1912

❑	9041	Silver	£25-30

Ref.	Model	Price Guide

1960s RE-ISSUES
Bentley 3L
❏	C861/1	Green	£5
❏	C861/2	Dk red	£5
❏	C861/3	Black	£5
❏	99076	Pewter	£14

Model T Ford
❏	C863/1	Black, black canopy	£5
❏	C863/2	Blue, black canopy	£5
❏	C863/3	Red, white canopy	£5

Renault 12/16
❏	C862/1	Yellow, black hood	£5
❏	C862/2	Brown, black hood	£5
❏	C862/3	Light blue, white hood	£5

Rolls Royce Silver Ghost
❏	C860/1	Silver	£5
❏	C860/2	Black	£5
❏	C860/3	Dk red	£5

1:36 SCALE
Bentley R Type
❏	C815	White, black roof	£16
❏	C815	Black, white roof	£14
❏	C815	2-tone blue, black roof	£14
❏	C815/1	2-tone beige/cream, cream roof	£5-10

Chevrolet Bel-Air — **£5-10**
❏	C825	Red, white roof	£5-10
❏	C825/1	Black, white roof	£5-10
❏	C825/2	Lt blue, white roof	£5-10
❏	96570	Gold	£5-10
❏	96571	Blue, white roof	£5-10

Ford Thunderbird
❏	C801	Cream, tan hood (open rear window)	£5-10
❏	C801	Cream, tan hood (no rear window)	£5-10
❏	C801	Cream, orange hood	£5-10
❏	C801	Cream, black hood	£5-10
❏	C801	Cream/orange, open top	£5-10

Ref.	Model	Price Guide
❏ C810	Pink, open top	£5-10
❏ C810	White, lack hood	£5-10
❏ C810	Red/white, open top	£5-10
❏ C810/2	Black, open top	£5-10
Jaguar XK120		
❏ C803	Red, black top	£7-10
❏ C804	Cream, black top, RN 414	£7-10
❏ C804	Cream, black tonneau, RN 414	£7-10
❏ C819	White, black top, RN7	£7-10
❏ C819	Maroon, black top	£17
❏ C870	Green, black tonneau, RN6	£7-10
❏ C870	Green, black top	£7-10
❏ C816	Red, black tonneau, RN56	£7-10
MG TF		
❏ C812	Green, open top	£7-10
❏ C813	Red, black top	£7-10
❏ C813	Cream/maroon, black top	£7-10
❏ C869	Blue, black tonneau	£7-10
Mercedes 300SL Gullwing		
❏ C802	Red	£5-10
❏ C811	Silver	£5-10
Mercedes 300s		
❏ C805	Maroon, tan hood	£5-10
❏ C805	Grey, tan hood	£5-10
❏ C805	Grey, open top	£5-10
❏ C805	Grey, black hood	£5-10
❏ C805	2-tone brown, tan hood	£5-10
❏ C805	Brown, black hood	£5-10
❏ C806	Black, open top	£5-10
❏ C806	Black, white hood	£5-10
❏ C806	2-tone grey, open top	£24
❏ C806	Blue/grey, open top	£5-10
❏ C806	Blue/grey, black hood	£5-10
❏ C806/1	Dk red, tan hood	£5-10
❏ C806/1	Dk red, open top	£5-10
Rolls Royce Silver Dawn		
❏ C814	Red/black	£5-10

Ref.	Model	Price Guide
❏ C814/1	Silver/black	£5-10
❏ C814/1	Beige/cream	£5-10

1:43 SCALE
Ford Cortina

❏ D708/1	White, green stripe (UK Made)	£8-10
❏ D708/2	Maroon	£8-10
❏ D708/3	Red	£8-10
❏ D708/4	Aqua	£8-10
❏ D708/7	Black	£8-10
❏ D708/8	Green	£8-10
❏ 1301	Grey, red stripe	£8-10
❏ 1302	RAC Rally 1966 - Jim Clark, RN8	£8-10
❏ 96501	Blue	£8-10
❏ 96502	Corgi Rally	£8-10
❏ 96760	Red/brown - John Whitmore, RN27	£8-10
❏ 96763	Red - Roger Clark, RN1	£8-10
❏ 96764	White, green stripe - Jim Clark, RN21	£8-10
❏ 98130	White, green stripe (Made in China)	£8-10
❏ 98165	London Transport	£8-10

Ford Popular

❏ C701/1	Grey	£8-10
❏ C701/3	Black (UK made)	£8-10
❏ C701/5	Fawn	£8-10
❏ C701/7	Green	£8-10
❏ C701/8	Newark grey	£8-10
❏ C701/9	Winchester blue	£8-10
❏ 1401	White	£8-10
❏ 1402	Black/red (FORD number plate)	£8-10
❏ 96481	Sage green	£8-10
❏ 98132	Black (made in China)	£8-10

Ford Zephyr

❏ D710/1	Black	£8-10
❏ D710/2	blue	£8-10
❏ D710/3	Red	£8-10
❏ D710/4	Grey	£8-10
❏ D710/6	Maroon	£8-10
❏ D710/7	Pompador blue	£8-10
❏ 96721	White - Ann Hall, RN85	£8-10
❏ 98133	Red, chrome detailing	£8-10

Ref.	Model	Price Guide
Ford Zodiac		
❏ D709/1	Maroon/grey	£8-10
❏ D709/2	2-tone blue	£8-10
❏ D709/3	Yellow/white	£8-10
❏ D709/4	Red/white	£8-10
❏ D709/6	Black/blue	£8-10
❏ D709/7	2-tone green. Classic Models presentation box	£11
❏ 1601	White/blue	£8-10
❏ 1602	Yellow/white (ZODIAC number plate)	£8-10
❏ 98135	Yellow/white	£8-10
Jaguar Mk2		
❏ C700/1	Red	£8-10
❏ C700/3	Black	£8-10
❏ C700/4	Metallic fawn	£8-10
❏ C700/5	Green	£8-10
❏ C700/6	Metallic blue	£8-10
❏ C700/7	Metallic grey	£8-10
❏ C700/8	Silver blue	£8-10
❏ C700/9	Willow green	£8-10
❏ 1802	Bronze	£8-10
❏ 1804	British racing green (JAGUAR number plate)	£8-10
❏ 1805	Gold plated 40th Anniversary model	£8-10
❏ 96680	Dk blue - Stirling Moss, RN36	£8-10
❏ 96683	White	£8-10
❏ 96685	White - Staffordshire Police	£8-10
❏ 96881	White - John Cobbs, RN16	£8-10
❏ CC01801	British Racing Green	£8-10
SAAB 96		
❏ D711	Red (renumbered 99045)	£8-10
❏ D711	Blue	£8-10
❏ D712	Maroon - Erik Carllson, RN283	£8-10
❏ 1701	Red (SAAB number plate)	£8-10
❏ 96662	Lt blue - Pat Moss, RN5	£8-10
Mercedes Benz 300SL Roadster		
❏ 3401	Green, open top	£8-10
❏ 3501	Black, soft top	£8-10
❏ 96410	Red, open top	£8-10
❏ 96411	Grey, open top	£8-10
❏ 96415	Ivory, black top	£8-10
❏ 96416	Silver, black top	£8-10

Ref.	Model	Price Guide

Morris Minor

	Ref.	Model	Price Guide
❏	C702/1	Black - Motoring School	£8-10
❏	C702/2	Dk blue	£8-10
❏	C702/4	Lilac	£8-10
❏	C702/5	Maroon - grey radiator surround	£8-10
❏		Maroon - maroon radiator surround	£8-10
❏	C702/6	Almond green	£8-10
❏	C702/7	Ivory	£8-10
❏	C702/8	Clipper blue	£8-10
❏	1901	Dk grey, red stripe	£8-10
❏	2002	Gold plated	£8-10
❏	96740	Cream - Pat Moss, RN121	£8-10
❏	96741	Dk blue - Himalayan Rally, RN67	£8-10
❏	96742	Ivory - London to Peking	£8-10
❏	96745	Black, red stripe	£8-10
❏	96746	Red - Rally, RN323	£8-10
❏	96756	Bristol Omnibus	£8-10

Morris Minor Convertible

	Ref.	Model	Price Guide
❏	2001	Grey/blue, blue stripe	£8-10
❏	96750	White	£8-10
❏	96751	Clipper blue	£8-10
❏	96752	Porcelain green	£8-10
❏	96753	Grey/blue, blue stripe	£8-10
❏	96754	Yellow	£8-10
❏	96755	Rose	£8-10
❏	96765	Almond green	£8-10
❏	97345	Black	£8-10

Morris Minor Traveller

	Ref.	Model	Price Guide
❏	2201	Blue	£8-10
❏	2202	Red	£8-10
❏	96870	Dk green	£8-10
❏	96871	Black	£8-10

Mini Cooper

	Ref.	Model	Price Guide
❏	98136	Almond green/white	£8-10
❏	98137	Black	£8-10
❏	98138	British racing green/white	£8-10
❏	98139	Red/white	£8-10
❏	98141	Police - Liverpool	£8-10

Pair of Leyland's from the Passage of Time series.
Sold for £48 DJ Auctions

4 American Fire engines including Seagraves (2),
E-One & E-side. Sold for £35 DJ Auctions

Ref.	Model	Price Guide
Austin Healey 3000		
☐ D733/1	White, red top	£8-10
☐ D734/1	Metallic blue, open top (renumbered 99050)	£8-10
☐ D735/1	Green, grey soft top	£8-10
☐ 2301	Colorado red, hard top	£8-10
☐ 2401	Black/yellow, soft top	£8-10
☐ 2501	Black/ivory, open top	£8-10
☐ 96200	Turquoise, white hard top	£8-10
☐ 96220	Metallic blue/ivory, open top	£8-10
☐ 96240	Yellow, open top	£8-10
Ferrari 250 GTO		
☐ D739/1	Red, RN151	£8-10
☐ D740/1	Red (renumbered 96320)	£8-10
☐ 2601	Yellow	£8-10
Jaguar E Type		
☐ 2701	Dk Green, open top	£8-10
☐ 2702	Maroon, open top	£8-10
☐ 2801	Black, soft top	£8-10
☐ 96042	Cream, black soft top	£8-10
☐ 96043	Black, open top	£8-10
☐ 96080	Red, open top	£8-10
☐ 96081	Yellow, open top	£8-10
☐ 96082	Gold - Ken Baker	£8-10
☐ 98120	Green, black soft top	£8-10
☐ 98121	Silver blue, open top	£8-10
Jaguar XK120		
☐ 2901	Racing Green, open top	£8-10
☐ 2902	Lavender, open top	£8-10
☐ 2903	Gold plated, open top	£8-10
☐ 3001	Grey, soft top	£8-10
☐ 96040	White, open top	£8-10
☐ 96041	Racing Green, open top	£8-10
☐ 96044	Maroon, white soft top	£8-10
☐ 96060	Black, white soft top	£8-10
MGA		
☐ D730/1	Silver, black hard top	£8-10
☐ D731/1	Racing Green, open top	£8-10
☐ D732/1	Red, black soft top (renumbered 99048)	£8-10

4 American La France Fire Engines.
Sold for £40 DJ Auctions

3 Famous Haulier series models including
Scammell tanker, Scammell Dropside & AEC Box
Trailer. Sold for £35 DJ Auctions

Ref.	Model	Price Guide
❏ 3101	Beige, hard top	£8-10
❏ 3201	Iris blue, soft top	£8-10
❏ 3301	Red, open top	£8-10
❏ 96140	Red, hard top	£8-10
❏ 96160	Black, open top	£8-10
❏ 96180	White, grey soft top	£8-10
Porsche 356B		
❏ D741/1	Red, black hard top	£8-10
❏ D742/1	White, open top	£8-10
❏ D743/1	Black, soft top	£8-10
❏ 3701	White, soft top	£8-10
❏ 3801	Red, open top	£8-10
❏ 96360	Royal blue, open top	£8-10
❏ 98123	Silver, open top	£8-10
Range Rover (1:36 Scale)		
❏ 57606	Gold 30th Anniversary model	£24
Triumph TR3A		
❏ D736/1	Red, black hard top	£8-10
❏ D737/1	Pale blue, open top	£8-10
❏ D738/1	Yellow, black soft (renumbered 99054)	£8-10
❏ 3901	Racing Green, hard top	£8-10
❏ 4001	White, soft top	£8-10
❏ 4101	Black, open top	£8-10
❏ 96300	Red, black soft top	£8-10
Ford Consul (1:36 Scale)		
❏ AN01101	Brown 50th anniversary model	£20
❏ AN01102	Bare casting 50th Anniversary model	NPA
❏ AN01103	Gold plated 50th Anniversary model	NPA
❏ AN01104	Great Book of Corgi model	£14
❏ AN01105	Chrome plated 50th Anniversary model	£24
❏ AN01106	Winchester Blue	NPA

1:36 SCALE
Mini (Various sponsor liveries)

❏ 4401	Viking Tyres	£5-10
❏ 4402	Corgi Classics	£5-10
❏ 4404	Gislaved	£5-10
❏ 4405	40th Anniversary model	£5-10

6 Corgi Collection Mini's including Equinox,
Charcoal. Flame Red, Monte Carlo, Kingfisher Blue
& Racing Green. Sold for £38 DJ Auctions

Thorneycroft J type Bus from the BP
collection made in Great Britain.
Sold for £8 Toy Price Guide Archive

Ref.	Model	Price Guide
❑ 4406	Rover	£5-10
❑ 4407	1994 Monte Carlo Rally RN 37	£5-10
❑ 4408	1996 Monte Carlo Rally	£5-10
❑ 4409	Equinox	£5-10
❑ 4410	Red	£5-10
❑ 4411	Mud splashed safari livery	£5-10
❑ 4412	Charcoal	£5-10
❑ 4413	Racing Green	£5-10
❑ 4414	Nurburgring	£5-10
❑ 4415	Eddie Stobart	£17
❑ 4416	Kingfisher Blue	£5-10
❑ 4417	HSS Anniversary	£5-10
❑ 4418	1994 Monte Carlo Rally RN 87	£5-10
❑ 4420	Cadbury's Mini Eggs	£5-10
❑ 4421	Non mud splashed safari livery	£5-10
❑ 4422	1997 Monte Carlo Rally	£5-10
❑ 4423	Mighty Mini Rally	£5-10
❑ 4424	1994 RAC Rally	£5-10
❑ 4425	1998 Ralleye de Espana	£5-10
❑ 4426	1998/9 Mintex Rally	£5-10
❑ 4427	1997 RAC Rally	£5-10
❑ 4428	Mighty Mini (Stephen King)	£5-10
❑ 4429	Mighty Mini (John Kirby)	£5-10
❑ 4430	Mighty Mini (Peter Crewes)	£5-10
❑ 4431	Mighty Mini (Sam Poach)	£5-10
❑ 4432	Mighty Mini (Nigel Ainge)	£5-10
❑ 4433	1998 Network Q RAC Rally	£5-10
❑ 4434	Mighty Mini Racing	£5-10
❑ 4435	Plant Brothers Millenium Mini	£5-10
❑ 4436	Mighty Mini (Chris Hunter)	£5-10
❑ 4437	Mighty Mini (Stewart Jenner)	£5-10
❑ 4439	Mini 7 (Tony Ragona)	£5-10
❑ 4444	Plant Brother, Jungle.com model	£5-10
❑ 4501	Gold plated 40th Anniversary model	£5-10
❑ 4502	Mulberry	£5-10
❑ 4503	White	£5-10
❑ 4504	Island Blue	£5-10
❑ 4505	Mini 40 (John Cooper)	£5-10
❑ 4506	Mighty Mini (Terry Colley)	£5-10
❑ 4507	Red/white Mini 40	£5-10
❑ 4509	Mini 40, End of the Road	£5-10
❑ 5508	Mini Se7en Racing Club diorama	£5-10

Q953/8 Bedford O Series Pantechnicon, 4000
Limited Edition Michael Gerson livery in grey box
complete with certificate & 2-fold mini leaflet.
Sold for £17 Toy Price Guide Archive

C897/8 AEC Forward Control 5 ton Cabover,
HMV livery in grey box.
Sold for £14 Toy Price Guide Archive

Ref.	Model	Price Guide
❏ CC82201	Knightsbridge Classic Edition	£5-10
❏ CC82202	Mini Se7en Racing Club (Steve Bell)	£5-10
❏ CC82203	Mini Se7en Racing Club (Chris Huck)	£5-10
❏ CC82204	Manx Rally (Eddie Stobart)	£5-10
❏ CC82205	Cooper S Amaranth, Classic Edition	£5-10
❏ CC82206	Mulberry Mini 40	£5-10
❏ CC82207	White Mini 40	£5-10
❏ CC82208	Blue Mini 40	£5-10
❏ CC82209	Rover Cooper sports Mini 40	£5-10
❏ CC82210	Gold plated	£5-10
❏ CC82211	Mini Se7en Racing Club (Pete Baldwin)	£5-10
❏ CC82212	Mini Se7en Racing Club (Dave Braggins)	£5-10
❏ CC82213	Harrods (Union Jack roof)	£5-10
❏ CC82214	Mini 40 (Ian Gunn)	£5-10
❏ CC82216	Mini 40 (Dave Banwell)	£5-10
❏ CC82219	Gold plated, red seats	£5-10
❏ CC82221	Black (Dave Kimberley)	£5-10
❏ CC82222	XVII Commonwealth Games	£5-10
❏ CC82223	Mini Ecosse	£5-10
❏ CC82225	Acropolis Rally, 2003 Club model	£5-10
❏ CC82226	Cadbury, Beachdean Diaries	£5-10
❏ CC82226	Cadbury, Beachdean Diaries (factory error)	£32
❏ CC82227	Cadbury RN 99 (Andrew Howard)	£5-10
❏ CC82228	Mini Maglia Canadian GT (Dyrk Bolger)	£5-10
❏ CC82230	Mini Magazine promotional	£5-10
❏ CC82231	Classic Edition	£5-10
❏ CC82232	Chris Lewis	£5-10
❏ CC82233	Mini 7 (Tim Sims)	£5-10
❏ CC82234	Green/white	£5-10
❏ CC82235	Blue/white	£5-10
❏ CC82236	Grey/white	£5-10
❏ CC82237	Dave Kimberley	£5-10
❏ CC82238	Sarah Munns	£5-10
❏ CC82239	Mini 7 (Bill Sollis)	£5-10
❏ CC82240	British Rally (Neil Burgess)	£5-10
❏ CC82241	Mini 7 Racing Club (James Hall)	£5-10
❏ CC82242	Monte Carlo Ralleye 2005 (Robert Stacey)	£5-10
❏ CC82243	Mini 7 Racing Club (Kelly Rogers)	£5-10
❏ CC82244	Dunlop	£5-10
❏ CC82245	Bill Sollis	£5-10
❏ CC82246	Peter Baldwin	£5-10
❏ CC82249	Peter Thompson	£5-10

BMW New mini Diorama (3 models) set.
Sold for £30 DJ Auctions

MacFarlane MAN TGA Curtainside & Bassett Scania
Curtainside. Sold for £60 DJ Actions

Ref.	Model	Price Guide
❑ CC82250	Rob Stacey	£5-10
❑ CC82251	Colin Peacock	£5-10
❑ CC82252	Chequered Classic Mini	£5-10
❑ CC99109	The Last Cooper S (3 mini plinth mounted set)	£17
❑ CC99153	Land Rover & Mini Seven on Trailer, Acropolis Rally 2004	£12
❑ CC99175	Tartan red Austin Mini & purple BMW Mini (Lord Mayors Show 2004)	£12
❑ CC99180	Racing Club 2pce set (Ian Curley)	£14
❑ CC99196	Mini Rally winter diorama set	£16

New Mini

Ref.	Model	Price Guide
❑ CC86501	Red	£5-10
❑ CC86502	Silver	£5-10
❑ CC86503	Black	£5-10
❑ CC86504	Yellow	£5-10
❑ CC86505	Orange	£5-10
❑ CC86506	Racing green	£5-10
❑ CC86508	2002 Club model	£5-10
❑ CC86509	Superchips	£5-10
❑ CC86510	Red - Teng Tools	£5-10
❑ CC86511	Red, John Cooper Challenge RN 2	£5-10
❑ CC86512	Blue, John Cooper Challenge RN 1 (Mike Cooper)	£5-10
❑ CC86513	John Cooper Challenge RN 12 (Dave Elliot) Fat Face	£5-10
❑ CC86515	Eddie Stobart	£5-10
❑ CC86516	NSW Police	£5-10
❑ CC86517	Royal Canadian Police	£5-10
❑ CC86518	Munich Police	£5-10
❑ CC86519	Durham Constabluary	£5-10
❑ CC86521	1964 Monte Carlo Rally, 40th Anniversary	£5-10
❑ CC86522	St Andrews flag	£5-10
❑ CC86523	St Georges	£5-10
❑ CC86524	Welsh Dragon	£5-10
❑ CC86525	Irish Tricolour	£5-10
❑ CC86526	Checkmate	£5-10
❑ CC86527	One Seven	£5-10
❑ CC86528	Park Lane	£5-10
❑ CC99121	3 BMW Mini Coopers (plinth mounted)	£27

LT1 Taxi

Ref.	Model	Price Guide
❑ CC95902	2002 Manchester Commonwealth Games	£5-10
❑ CC85903	Golden Jubilee	£5-10

Mercedes Actros pair; Pulleyn & Southbar Transport. Sold for £40 DJ Auctions

Group of 5 1:50th scale modern trucks. Sold for £48 DJ Auctions

Ref.	Model	Price Guide
GIFT SETS		
D16/1	Racing Fords 3pce set (Popular, Cortina & Zodiac)	£17
D36/1	Racing Zephyrs 3pce set	£16
D53/1	Rally 3pce set (Jaguar mk2, Austin Healey & MGA)	£19
5505	CSMA 75th Anniversary (Jaguar XK120, Model T ford, Capri & Morris Minor)	£12
5508	Mini Se7en Racing Club 2pce diorama set	£15
97680	E Type Jaguar 30th Anniversary 2pce set	£15
97681	Stirling's Choice (Jaguary XK120 & Austin Healey)	£25-30
97690	Ferrari 250GT 3pce set	£14
97695	Abingdon 3pce set (2 x MGA's & Morris J Van)	£19
97700	Jaguar through the Ages 3pce set (E Type, XK120 & Mk2)	£37
97701	Racing E Types 2pce set	£17
97702	The Jaguar Collection 3pce set (plinth mounted)	£30-35
97703	RAC Rally 3pce XK120 set	£35-40
97706	First Time Out 3pce XK120 set	£19
97708	Tour de France 3pce set (Jaguar, Ferrari & Mini Cooper)	£22
97709	Alpine Rally 3pce set (Austin Healey, Cortina & Mini Cooper)	£22
97712	Monte Carlo 3pce set	£32
97730	Austin Healey Winners 3pce set	£19
RACING CARS		
DONINGTON COLLECTION (re-issue of 1970s models)		
97373	Hesketh 308	£10-13
97374	Surtees TS9	£10-13
97375	Shadow DN1	£10-13
97376	Ferrari 312B	£10-13
97377	Lotus 72D	£10-13
97378	Surtees TS9B	£10-13
Legends of Speed		
201	Green	£5-10
202	Blue	£5-10
203	Silver	£5-10

3 unboxed Tractor Units including
Scania, Mercedes & DAF.
Sold for £30 DJ Auctions

A pair of C897/6 AEC 5 Ton Forward Control
Cabover Forward in Weetabix livery.
Sold for £14 Toy Price Guide Archive

Ref.	Model	Price Guide

COMMERCIALS

AEC Cabover Van

☐ C897/1	Carter Paterson/Atora	£8-12
☐ C897/2	John Knight/Hustler	£8-12
☐ C897/3	LMS Parcels	£16
☐ C897/4	Duckhams	£8-12
☐ C897/5	Amplion	£8-12
☐ C897/6	Weetabix	£8-12
☐ C897/7	Mars	£8-12
☐ C897/8	HMV	£8-12
☐ C897/9	International Stores	£8-12
☐ C897/10	Potters Asthma Cure	£8-12
☐ C897/11	John Barker	£8-12
☐ C897/12	Royal Mail	£8-12
☐ C897/14	GWR	£8-12
☐ 97140	Southern Railway	£8-12

AEC Cabover Tanker

☐ C945/1	Flowers	£8-12
☐ C945/2	Gaymers	£8-12
☐ C945/3	Carles Capel	£8-12
☐ C945/4	Duckhams	£8-12
☐ C945/5	Somerlite Oil	£8-12
☐ C945/6	Redline	£8-12
☐ C945/9	Mobilgas	£8-12
☐ C945/10	BP	£8-12

1:50 SCALE
AEC Ergomatic

☐ 20801	Johnnie Walker tanker	£20-25
☐ 20901	Trumans	£20-25
☐ 20903	Eddie Stobart	£20-25
☐ 21101	Guinness tanker	£34
☐ 21201	Mackintosh's	£20-25
☐ 21301	Ferrymasters	£27
☐ 21302	Caledonian	£20-25
☐ 21303	Bells Whisky	£20-25
☐ 21401	Walls Ice Cream refrigerated box trailer	£20-25
☐ 21402	Daniel Stewart	£20-25
☐ 21501	Limmer & Trinidad dropside	£20-25

Ian Hayes pair; Scania Topline Curtainside
& Scania T Cab Tanker.
Sold for £95 DJ Auctions

Tate & Lyle boxed set.
Sold for £19 Toy Price Guide Archive

Ref.	Model	Price Guide
❏ 21601	Eddie Stobart tipper	£31
❏ 22201	BRS	£29
❏ 31003	Chris Miller	£45
❏ 97328	Major tanker	£20-25
❏ 97369	Eddie Stobart truck & trailer	£20-25
❏ 97370	Federation Ales	£20-25
❏ 97894	Pickfords (Ltd Ed 5000)	£18
❏ 97895	BRS	£22
❏ 97931	Greenhall Whitley	£22
❏ 97932	NE Gas Board tanker	£20
❏ CC10301	Willmotts	£35-40
❏ CC10302	BRS	£32
❏ CC10309	Pollocks	£20-25

AEC Mk5 Mammoth Major

❏ 26401	London Brick Co.(Ltd Ed 5000)	£34
❏ 26402	BRS	£24-28
❏ 26403	Henry Long, wool bale load (Ltd Ed 3000)	£24-28
❏ 26404	Eddie Stobart (Ltd Ed 5000)	£22
❏ 26601	Newhouse tipper	£24-28
❏ 26701	Guinness tanker (Ltd Ed 6000)	£22
❏ CC11501	Siddle Cook	£24-28
❏ CC11502	Shell BP tanker	£24-28
❏ CC11503	BRS	£24-28
❏ CC11504	Spiers	£35-40
❏ CC11505	Smith of Maddiston	£40-50
❏ CC11507	Suttons	£40-50
❏ CC11508	Smiles & Co	£40-50
❏ CC11509	Nuttall & Sons Ltd	£35

Albion Caledonian

❏ 26001	Ballantines, box van	£24
❏ 26201	TW Davidson	£24

Albion Ergomatic cab

❏ 21001	White Horse	£20-25
❏ 26101	Ward (Ltd Ed 4000)	£20-25
❏ 26101	Tyson Burridge	£20-25

Albion LAD

❏ 23601	Robsons of Carlisle	£30-35
❏ 23602	Eddie Stobart	£30-35

Ref.	Model	Range	Price Guide
❑ 23801	LBC, Phorpes brick load		£34
❑ 23802	Post Office Supplies		£33
❑ CC11602	BRS		£30-35
❑ CC11603	Malcolm		£42
❑ CC11607	Richards		£30-35
❑ CC11608	Russell of Bathgate		£30-35
❑ CC11610	Pollock		£37
❑ CC11611	Pollock		£30-35

Atkinson 8-wheel rigid

Ref.	Model		Price Guide
❑ 27201	Fina tanker		£18
❑ 27301	Bulwark tanker		£15
❑ 27501	Aaron Henshaw		£16
❑ 27601	FB Atkins		£33
❑ 27701	Whitbread		£25-30
❑ 27901	Vaux Beers tanker		£25-30
❑ 28001	Suttons		£25-30
❑ 28101	DM Smith		£25-30
❑ 28201	Gibb's		£25-30
❑ 97162	Pollock		£17
❑ 97327	Stobart		£33
❑ 97334	Lucozade		£25-30
❑ 97366	Tennants		£25-30
❑ 97372	Mackeson tanker		£25-30

Atkinson Borderer

Ref.	Model		Price Guide
❑ CC12501	Riding		£35-45
❑ CC12502	Eddie Stobart (Ltd Ed 6200)		£35-45
❑ CC12503	Gibbs		£35-45
❑ CC12504	Pollock		£35-45
❑ CC12505	Richard Preston		£35-45
❑ CC12508	Killingbeck		£35-45
❑ CC12509	Bassetts Roadways		£35-45
❑ CC12510	WH Bowker		£35-45
❑ CC12512	British Rail		£35-45

Atkinson Venturer

Ref.	Model		Price Guide
❑ CC11405	BRS		£35-45
❑ CC12506	Wynns		£35-45
❑ CC12507	Pickfords		£35-45
❑ CC12513	JB Rawcliffe		£35-45

Bedford O Articulated

Ref.	Model		Price Guide
❑ 18401	British Rail		£15-20
❑ 18402	Terry's		£15-20
❑ 18403	British Railways		£27
❑ 18404	HE Musgrove		£37
❑ 18801	Eddie Stobart (KM)		£25
❑ 97329	BRS		£15-20
❑ 97301	London Brick Co		£15-20

Bedford O Box Van

Ref.	Model		Price Guide
❑ C822/1	Persil		£14
❑ C822/2	Tate & Lyle		£16
❑ C822/3	Gillette		£14
❑ C822/4	Carter Patterson, green roof		£12-15
❑ C822/4	Carter Patterson, red roof		£25-30
❑ C822/5	Millers Baking powder		£11
❑ C822/7	Cadbury's		£10-15
❑ C822/8	Maltesers		£10-15
❑ C822/10	Terry's		£10-15
❑ C822/11	LNER		£10-15

Ref.	Model	Range	Price Guide
❑ C822/12	Toymaster		£5
❑ 97120	LMS		£22
❑ 97123	NSPCC		£15-20
❑ 97124	Youngsters		£15-20
❑ 97125	Post Office Telephones		£15-20
❑ 97126	NCB		£15-20
❑ 97371	Cameron Breweries		£15-20

Bedford O Pantechnicon

Ref.	Model	Range	Price Guide
❑ C953/1	Pickfords		£7
❑ C953/2	Waring & Gillows		£27
❑ C953/3	Frasers of Ipswich		£17
❑ C953/4	Steinway & Sons		£21
❑ C953/5	Griff Fender		£10-15
❑ C953/6	Duckhams		£7
❑ C953/7	Camp Hopson		£10-15
❑ C953/8	Michael Gerson		£10-15
❑ C953/9	Stylo		£10-15
❑ C953/10	Weetabix		£10-15
❑ C953/12	Bishops		£10-15
❑ C953/13	Wylie & Lochhead		£10-15
❑ C953/14	Arthur Batty		£10-15
❑ C953/16	Lee Brothers, green wheels		£10-15
❑ C953/16	Lee Brothers, silver wheels		£10-15
❑ 18301	Watts Bros		£10-15
❑ 18302	Elite International		£10-15
❑ 97080	John Julian		£10-15
❑ 97081	Brewer & Turnbull		£10-15
❑ 97084	Grattons		£15
❑ 97085	Slumberlands		£14
❑ 97086	Freeborns		£12
❑ 97087	Barnardos		£10-15
❑ 97088	White & Co		£10-15
❑ 97089	John Mason		£10-15
❑ 97090	Rileys		£10-15
❑ 97091	Lucking & Sons		£10-15
❑ 97093	Happy Birthday (standard issue)		£10-15
❑ 97093	Happy Birthday (Corgi Heritage Centre issue)		£10-15
❑ 97195	Howells		£10-15
❑ 97602	Pickfords		£10-15
❑ -	Gold plate version		£27
❑ CC60307	Bedford QLD Lime spreader, BRS		£20

Bedford S

Ref.	Model	Range	Price Guide
❑ 19201	Cambridgeshire Emergency Tender	Golden Oldies	£18
❑ 19301	Lyons	Golden Oldies	£15-20
❑ 19302	Weetabix	Golden Oldies	£15-20
❑ 19304	Walls	Archive Corgi	£15-20
❑ 19306	Eddie Stobart		£15-20
❑ -	Royal Worcester		£15-20
❑ 19401	Ken Thomas		£15-20
❑ 19601	Worthington Bass		£15-20
❑ 19701	AFS		£15-20
❑ 19702	Tetley		£25
❑ 19801	Eddie Stobart (Ltd Ed 6600)		£27
❑ 19802	JW Richards		£15-20
❑ 19901	BRS		£27
❑ 20001	W & J Riding		£15-20
❑ 20201	Esso tanker		£15-20
❑ 20202	Milk tanker	Archive Corgi	£15-20
❑ 20301	British Railways		£32
❑ 20401	Laing tipper	Building Britain	£15-20

❏ 20501	Pickfords		£15-20
❏ 30303	Spratts	Golden Oldies	£15-20
❏ 31004	Wynns	Heavy Haulage	£42
❏ CC10901	County of Clwyd		£15-20
❏ CC10902	BRS		£15-20

Bedford TK

❏ 22401	British Railways (Ltd Ed 5000)		£18
❏ 22402	Garrett steam engine on low loader (Ltd Ed 5000)	Vintage Glory	£37
❏ 22501	BRS		£20-25
❏ 22502	MacBraynes		£20-25
❏ 22503	Guinness		£20-25
❏ 22504	Guinness		£42
❏ 22601	Cabdury's tanker		£37
❏ 22701	Pickfords		£18
❏ 22702	Eddie Stobart (Ltd Ed 5000)		£20-25
❏ 22704	Guinness		£20-25
❏ 22705	BT		£20-25
❏ 22706	Guinness		£20-25
❏ 22801	Shell BP tanker		£31
❏ 22901	Tarmac tipper	Building Britain	£20-25
❏ 22902	Blue Circle Cement	Building Britain	£20-25
❏ 23201	Guinness		£20-25
❏ 23202	Whitbread		£20-25
❏ 23203	Eddie Stobart		£20-25
❏ CC11401	Pickfords		£36
❏ CC11406	Pickfords		£20-25
❏ CC11407	Hoults		£20-25
❏ CC11408	Ulster Transport		£20-25
❏ CC11408	Pickfords		£20-25
❏ CC11409	McMullen Gladstone Bitter		£20-25
❏ CC11412	Walkers of Wakefield	On the Move	£20-25
❏ CC11415	J Beasley	Marquis of Distinction	£20-25
❏ CC11416	Pollock	Road Transport Heritage	£20-25

BMC

❏ CC13301	Eddie Stobart		£17
❏ CC13302	BRS		£20-25
❏ CC13303	Bishops Move		£20-25
❏ CC13304	Watneys		£20-25
❏ CC13305	Whitbread		£20-25
❏ CC13306	British Rail		£20-25
❏ CC13307	Brewer & Turnbull		£20-25
❏ CC13308	BRS		£20-25
❏ CC13309	Brickwoods Ales	Road Transport Heritage	£20-25
❏ CC13310	Gaymers Cider	Road Transport Heritage	£20-25
❏ CC13311	E Lacon & Co Ltd	Road Transport Heritage	£20-25

DAF CF

❏ CC13601	B Swain & Sons	Hauliers of Renown	£30-40
❏ CC13602	Suttons	Hauliers of Renown	£30-40
❏ CC13603	Tyson H Burridge Ltd	Hauliers of Renown	£30-40
❏ CC13604	RMC Aggregates		£30-40
❏ CC13605	Charlie Lauder Transport		£30-40
❏ CC13606	Drysdale Freight	Hauliers of Renown	£30-40
❏ CC13607	JC Ball tipper		£30-40
❏ CC13608	Kettlewels tipper	Hauliers of Renown	£30-40
❏ CC13609	Thomas Armstrong		£37
❏ CC13610	AK Londston	Hauliers of Renown	£50
❏ CC13611	Pollock		£42
❏ CC13612	James S Hislop	Hauliers of Renown	£50
❏ CC13613	Longs of Leeds		£42

Ref.	Model	Range	Price Guide
❑ CC13614	P McKerral & Co	Hauliers of Renown	£50
❑ CC13615	Skeldons	Hauliers of Renown	£55-60
❑ CC13617	Trustwell	Hauliers of Renown	£55-60
❑ CC13618	HE Payne	Hauliers of Renown	£55-60
❑ CC13619	Tennant tipper	Hauliers of Renown	£55-60

DAF 105
❑ CC14101	Baybutt of Burscough	Hauliers of Renown	£50-60
❑ CC14102	Craib	Hauliers of Renown	£50-60
❑ CC14103	Lanes	Hauliers of Renown	£50-60

DAF XF
❑ CC13201	Eddie Stobart	Hauliers of Renown	£55
❑ CC13202	Longs of Leeds	Hauliers of Renown	£32
❑ CC13203	Allely's Ltd with locomotive load	Heavy Haulage	£45
❑ CC13204	De Rijke (dutch)		£19
❑ CC13205	Visbeen (dutch)		£20-30
❑ CC13206	Reids Transport	Hauliers of Renown	£20-30
❑ CC13207	Eddie Stobart		£20-30
❑ CC13208	Prestons of Potto	Hauliers of Renown	£15
❑ CC13209	TSL Van Guard Ltd 7pce set	Heavy Haulage	£79
❑ CC13210	Gibbs	Hauliers of Renown	£16
❑ CC13211	Downton	Hauliers of Renown	£20-30
❑ CC13212	Grimers	Hauliers of Renown	£20-30
❑ CC13213	Allely's Ltd	Heavy Haulage	£20-30
❑ CC13214	Woodside Haulage Ltd	Hauliers of Renown	£20-30
❑ CC13215	Houghton Parkhouse/Portsoy Livestock	Hauliers of Renown	£20-30
❑ CC13216	Wrefords	Hauliers of Renown	£20-30
❑ CC13217	Ramage	Hauliers of Renown	£20-30
❑ CC13218	Jack Richards	Truckfest series	£20-30
❑ CC13219	Tarmac PLC	Hauliers of Renown	£43
❑ CC13220	Robert Laidlaw		£20-30
❑ CC13221	Parsons		£20-30
❑ CC13222	William Nicol Transport	Hauliers of Renown	£20-30
❑ CC13223	EA Gill	Hauliers of Renown	£17
❑ CC13224	Longhorne of Hebden	Hauliers of Renown	£20-30
❑ CC13225	Chamberlain Transport	Hauliers of Renown	£20-30
❑ CC13226	Robert Walker		£20-30
❑ CC13227	LV Transport	Hauliers of Renown	£52
❑ CC13228	ARR Craib	Hauliers of Renown	£40-50
❑ CC13229	David Murray	Hauliers of Renown	£40-50
❑ CC13231	James Irlam	Hauliers of Renown	£40-50
❑ CC13232	Beamish Transport	Truckfest series	£40-50
❑ CC13233	Grampian Maclennans	Hauliers of Renown	£59
❑ CC13234	John G Russell	Hauliers of Renown	£56
❑ CC13235	Marshalls crane trailer		£56
❑ CC13237	JCB exhibition unit		£62
❑ CC13238	Tinnelly	Truckfest series	£36
❑ CC13239	Kinlochbervie fridge trailer		£59
❑ CC13240	Peter Wood	Hauliers of Renown	£40-50
❑ CC13241	McRitchie	Hauliers of Renown	£40-50
❑ CC13242	Leicester	Hauliers of Renown	£62
❑ CC13243	William C Hockin	Hauliers of Renown	£69

Diamond T
❑ 31007	Annis & Co, loco load	Heavy Haulage	£50-60
❑ 31009	Wynns	Heavy Haulage	£50-60
❑ 55201	Pickfords		£50-60
❑ 55501	Elliotts of York	Heavy Haulage	£25-30
❑ 55603	Cadzow	Heavy Haulage	£25-30
❑ 55604	BRS		£25-30
❑ 55605	Blackpool Transport		£25-30
❑ 55608	Watneys		£25-30

ERF V

Ref.	Model	Range	Price Guide
9601	BRS South Eastern		£45
9701	ERF Parts Dept		£24-28
9801	John Smith		£24-28
9802	Corgi Classics Ltd		£24-28
9803	BRS/Russells of Bathgate		£35-40
9804	W Holden		£35-40
10001	McEwans (Ltd Ed 4000)		£29
10101	BRS		£35-40
10102	Gwynne Bowen		£35-40
10103	Ken Thomas		£35-40
10201	BRS		£35-40
97319	Bass		£35-40
97930	Blue Circle		£35-40
97940	Eddie Stobart		£35-40
97942	Flowers		£35-40
97980	Esso		£35-40
CC10201	BRS		£35-40
CC10202	Pickfords		£35-40
CC10204	BRS		£35-40

ERF KV

Ref.	Model	Range	Price Guide
11001	Eddie Stobart		£32
11101	Moorhouses Jam	Archive Corgi	£15-20
1301	Russell of Bathgate		£30-35
11401	Black & White		£30-35
11501	Shell BP		£30-35
11601	Eddie Stobart (Ltd Ed 2700)		£42
11603	BRS		£30-35
11701	Blowers	Building Britain	£30-35
11801	Scottish & Newcastle		£50
11802	Bass Worthington		£30-35
11803	BRS		£30-35
31011	Robert Walker	Heavy Haulage	£30-35
CC10501	Richard Read		£30-35
CC10503	Pollock		£30-35
CC10504	Ketton Cement tipper		£37
CC10505	Ind Coupe		£30-35
CC10506	Rileys Transport	Marques of Distinction	£30-35
CC10507	Babycham	Road Transport Heritage	£30-35

ERF EC

Ref.	Model	Range	Price Guide
74901	Rugby Cement powder tanker		£30-35
74902	AJA Smith powder tanker		£30-35
74903	Castle Cement		£30-35
74904	WR Wood		£24
75001	Lynx		£30-35
75101	Gulf		£30-35
75102	Shell		£30-35
75103	BP		£30-35
75104	Esso		£30-35
75201	Eddie Stobart		£30-35
75202	Boddingtons		£30-35
75203	Richard Read		£30-35
75204	Richards & Sons		£55
75205	Pollock		£55
75206	Massey Wilcox		£55
CC11901	Brian Harris		£97
CC11902	Castle Cement		£45-55
CC11904	Redland		£45-55
CC11905	Jos Millican		£45-55
CC11906	JB McBean (Ltd Ed 4000)		£33

Ref.	Model	Range	Price Guide
❑ CC11907	BP		£45-55
❑ CC11908	AJ Nelson	Hauliers of Renown	£45-55
❑ CC11909	Bowring	Heavy Haulage	£45-55
❑ CC11910	Brian Harris	Hauliers of Renown	£45-55
❑ CC11912	KP Iddon	Hauliers of Renown	£45-55
❑ CC11913	Brian Harris		£45-55
❑ CC11914	JCB trailer & excavator		£45-55

ERF ECS

Ref.	Model	Range	Price Guide
❑ CC12701	ERF New Generation		£38-45
❑ CC12702	Stoford		£38-45
❑ CC12703	Vaughan Logistics		£23
❑ CC12704	WH Malcolm		£38-45
❑ CC12705	Jack Richards & Sons		£38-45
❑ CC12706	Stan Robinson		£29
❑ CC12707	Turners of Soham	Hauliers of Renown	£38-45
❑ CC12708	Jet tanker	Hauliers of Renown	£38-45
❑ CC12709	Blue Circle Cement	Hauliers of Renown	£38-45

ERF ECT High Entry Sleeper

Ref.	Model	Range	Price Guide
❑ CC13402	Torridge	Hauliers of Renown	£45-50
❑ CC13406	Saints, fleet no. STS117	Hauliers of Renown	£45-50
❑ CC13406E	Saints, fleet no. STS119	Hauliers of Renown	£60
❑ CC13407	Tarmac PLC	Hauliers of Renown	£45-50
❑ CC13408	Richard Read	Hauliers of Renown	£45-50
❑ CC13409	John Mitchell	Hauliers of Renown	£45-50
❑ CC13410	Pollock	Truckfest series	£24
❑ CC13411	RDL Distribution	Hauliers of Renown	£45-50
❑ CC13412	Gerry Jones	Hauliers of Renown	£45-50
❑ CC13413	McCilla		£45-50
❑ CC13414	Innovate Logistics	Hauliers of Renown	£38
❑ CC13415	Eddie Stobart	Hauliers of Renown	£33
❑ CC13416	Hanbury Davies	Hauliers of Renown	£45-50
❑ CC13417	Ian Wright	Truckfest series	£33
❑ CC13418	JR Adams 50th Anniversary model		£82
❑ CC13419	Gold plated 50th Anniversary model		£197
❑ CC13420	Woody's Express	Hauliers of Renown	£45-50
❑ CC13421	Sloan Transport	Hauliers of Renown	£45-50
❑ CC13422	Beck & Pollitzer		£82
❑ CC13423	RT Keedwell	Hauliers of Renown	£47
❑ CC13424	TP Niven milk tanker	Hauliers of Renown	£42
❑ CC13425	JCB low loader		£79
❑ CC13426	Evans Transport crane trailer	Hauliers of Renown	£79
❑ CC13427	Collett low loader with JCB & van load	Heavy Haulage	£82
❑ CC13428	Gault Haulage	Hauliers of Renown	£65-75
❑ CC13429	McFarlane	Hauliers of Renown	£65-75

Foden Alpha

Ref.	Model	Range	Price Guide
❑ CC13901	JH Jones & Sons		£39
❑ CC13902	R & H Scott	Hauliers of Renown	£40-50
❑ CC13903	Stan Robinson		£40-50
❑ CC13904	Woodhead Bros	Hauliers of Renown	£40-50
❑ CC13905	Henry Streeter Ltd		£40-50
❑ CC13906	Richie Transport	Hauliers of Renown	£40-50
❑ CC13908	Reids Transport	Truckfest series	£40-50
❑ CC13909	Stocks & Sons		£40-50
❑ CC13910	William Armstrong/Gretna FC	Hauliers of Renown	£40-50
❑ CC13911	JRJ & I Monkhouse	Hauliers of Renown	£40-50
❑ CC13912	Cadzow with Atkinson & Escort van	Heavy Haulage	£62
❑ CC13913	A & S Grant	Hauliers of Renown	£55-65

Ref.	Model	Range	Price Guide
Foden FG			
☐ 97309	BRS		£36
☐ 97317	S&N Breweries		£32
☐ 97950	Guinness		£50
☐ 97951	Milk Marketing Board		£21
☐ 97952	Hovis		£33-38
☐ 97955	Guinness/G&C Moore (Ltd Ed 7500)		£49
☐ 97956	Pickfords		£59
☐ 97970	Regent		£33-38
☐ 97971	Robsons of Carlisle		£33-38
☐ 12101	Cadbury's Dairy Milk		£33-38
☐ 12301	Motor Packing Co Ltd		£33-38
☐ 12302	Eastwoods	Building Britain	£50
☐ 12401	Fremlins		£33-38
☐ 12501	Blue Circle Cement		£18
☐ 12801	Edward Beck	Heavy Haulage	£33-38
☐ CC10101	Blue Circle Cement		£37
☐ CC10102	Kierby & Perry		£42
☐ CC10103	Silver Roadways Ltd		£38
Foden S21			
☐ 13501	Munton (Ltd Ed 7000)	Heavy Haulage	£25-30
☐ 13601	Eddie Stobart		£25-30
☐ 13602	CWS Soft Drinks	Archive Corgi	£25-30
☐ 13701	Arrow Bulk Carriers Ltd		£25-30
☐ 13901	Bassett Roadways Ltd		£25-30
☐ 13902	Knowles Transport	Heavy Haulage	£25-30
☐ 13903	British Railways		£25-30
☐ 13904	Blue Circle	Building Britain	£25-30
☐ 13905	Rugby Cement	Building Britain	£25-30
☐ 14001	H & R Johnson		£25-30
☐ 14301	Eddie Stobart		£25-30
☐ 14302	Eddie Stobart		£25-30
☐ 14303	Eddie Stobart		£25-30
☐ 14401	Hoveringham Gravels	Building Britain	£25-30
☐ 14501	Blue Circle Cement	Building Britain	£25-30
☐ CC10801	Moreton C Cullimore		£39
☐ CC10803	Sam Longson		£25-30
☐ CC10805	Eddie Stobart		£25-30
☐ CC10806	Richard Johnson & Nephew	Marques of Distinction	£25-30
Ford Transcontinental			
☐ 23001	Midlands BRS		£30-40
☐ 23101	Eddie Stobart		£30-40
☐ 23301	Pollock		£30-40
Ford Thames Trader			
☐ 19303	Heinz 57	Golden Oldies	£15-20
☐ 30101	Wimpey tipper	Building Britain	£15-20
☐ 30102	London Brick Co tipper		£15-20
☐ 30201	RA Kembert & Sons		£15-20
☐ 30202	Eddie Stobart		£15-20
☐ 30301	Slumberland	Golden Oldies	£15-20
☐ 30302	Ever Ready	Golden Oldies	£15-20
☐ 30304	Robsons		£15-20
☐ 30305	1997 Corgi Club model		£15-20
☐ 30306	Lucozade	Archive Corgi	£15-20
☐ 30307	AFS control unit		£15-20
☐ 30308	Fox's Glacier Mints		£15-20
☐ 30309	Pickfords		£15-20
☐ 30310	Cadbury's Bourneville		£15-20
☐ 30401	Gulf tanker		£15-20

Ref.	Model	Range	Price Guide
❑ 30501	Pickfords		£15-20
❑ CC11001	British Rail		£20-25
❑ CC11002	Robsons		£20-25
❑ CC11003	GW Jeakins	On the Move	£20-25

Guy Invincible

Ref.	Model	Range	Price Guide
❑ 29101	Blue Circle		£20-25
❑ 29102	Wynns		£20-25
❑ 29103	Eddie Stobart		£20-25
❑ 29104	Tarmac	Building Britain	£25
❑ 29105	WH Bowker		£25-35
❑ 29202	Russell of Bathgate		£25-35
❑ 29203	Shore Porter Society		£25-35
❑ 29301	Arthur R Duckett		£25-35
❑ 29401	Dawsons Fargo Ltd		£25-35
❑ 31014	Sunter Brothers	Heavy Haulage	£25-35
❑ CC11701	McGall & Greenshields		£25-35
❑ CC11702	Regent tanker		£25-35
❑ CC11704	Frederick Ray	Marques of Distinction	£25-35

Guy Warrior

Ref.	Model	Range	Price Guide
❑ 28901	BRS		£20-25
❑ 29001	Dee Valley Transport		£19
❑ 29201	BRS		£20-25
❑ 29501	Post Office Supplies		£35
❑ CC11703	Wynns		£35

Leyland Mouth Organ cab

Ref.	Model	Range	Price Guide
❑ 23501	Cadbury's Cocoa tipper		£20-25
❑ 24201	McKelvie & Co Ltd		£20-25
❑ 24202	Power (Ltd Ed 5500)		£20-25
❑ 24203	Shell BP		£20-25
❑ 24301	Youngers tanker with figures (Ltd Ed 10000)		£20-25
❑ 24302	Double Diamond		£20-25
❑ 24402	Eddie Stobart		£20-25
❑ 24501	J & A Smith		£20-25
❑ 24502	London Brick Co	Building Britain	£20-25
❑ 24503	Walter Southworth		£32
❑ 24601	BRS		£20-25
❑ 24701	Michelin		£20-25
❑ 24901	Guinness		£20-25
❑ 25001	British Railways		£20-25
❑ 25101	BRS		£20-25
❑ 25102	Eddie Stobart		£20-25
❑ 25201	Smiths of Eccles		£20-25
❑ 25401	W Hancock & Sons		£32
❑ CC10601	Caledonian Road Services Ltd		£25-30
❑ CC10602	EEC Ltd		£40
❑ CC10603	Edward Derbyshire	Marques of Distinction	£20-25
❑ CC10604	Gibbs of Fraserburgh	Marques of Distinction	£20-25
❑ CC10605	Rileys Transport	Marques of Distinction	£20-25
❑ CC10606	Pollock	Road Transport Heritage	£20-25

Leyland Ergonomic Cab

Ref.	Model	Range	Price Guide
❑ 20902	Guinness		£37
❑ 22101	BRS		£27
❑ 22302	Guinness		£40
❑ 25301	Holt Lane Transport		£15-20
❑ CC10308	Charles Alexander	Marques of Distinction	£32

Leyland LAD Cab

Ref.	Model	Range	Price Guide
❑ 23701	Guinness (Ltd Ed 7100)		£28

Ref.	Model	Range	Price Guide
❏ 23702	T Brady & Sons Ltd		£35-40
❏ 23901	Steel, Peech & Tozer		NPA
❏ CC11601	A Wishart & Sons		£35-40
❏ CC11604	Castrol tanker		£35-40
❏ CC11605	BRS low loader		£44
❏ CC11609	HB & H		£35-40

Leyland DAF 85

Ref.	Model	Range	Price Guide
❏ 75301	Q8 tanker		£35-40
❏ 75302	Jet tanker		£35-40
❏ 75401	James Irlam		£48
❏ 75402	Tate & Lyle		£35-40
❏ 75403	Eddie Stobart		£35-40
❏ 75404	Heineken		£21
❏ 75405	Knights of Old		£35-40
❏ 75406	Ken Thomas Ltd		£35-40
❏ 75407	Guinness		£35-40
❏ 75408	T Brady & Sons Ltd		£55
❏ 75501	Parcelforce		£35-40
❏ 75502	Royal Mail		£26
❏ 75901	Slag Cement ltd		£35-40
❏ 75902	Blue Circle		£35-40
❏ 75903	WH Higgins & Sons		£35-40
❏ CC11801	Clugston		£35-40
❏ CC11803	Spaansen BV (dutch)		£35-40
❏ CC11804	Hanson tipper		£35-40
❏ CC11805	Ernest Thorpe	Hauliers of Renown	£35-40
❏ 30901	Luffing Shovel, Wimpey	Building Britain	£16

Mack Vans

Ref.	Model	Range	Price Guide
❏ C906/1	Mack		£8-10
❏ C906/2	Sunshine Biscuits		£8-10
❏ C906/3	White Rock		£8-10
❏ C906/4	Buffalo Fire Dept		£8-10
❏ C906/5	Pepsi Cola		£8-10
❏ C906/6	Stanley Tools		£8-10
❏ C906/7	Peerless Light Co		£8-10
❏ C906/8	Bovril		£8-10
❏ C906/9	Carnation		£8-10
❏ C906/10	Guddens Mustard		£8-10
❏ 98481	Greyhound Express Van Service		£8-10

MAN

Ref.	Model	Range	Price Guide
❏ 75701	TNT		£25
❏ 75702	Eddie Stobart		£40-45
❏ 75801	MAN Race Power (German)		£40-45
❏ 75802	Continental (German)		£40-45
❏ 75803	Gallachers		£40-45
❏ 75804	Eddie Stobart		£40-45
❏ 75805	Safegard (Ltd Ed 1900)		£31
❏ 75806	WH Malcolm Ltd		£40-45
❏ 75807	John Raymond Transport		£67
❏ 76201	Aral (German)		£40-45
❏ 76301	Rohbach Zement (German)		£40-45
❏ 76801	Stiller Transport		£40-45
❏ 76802	Dunkerley Transport	Heavy Haulage	£40-45
❏ CC12001	John Mitchell curtainsider		£35-45
❏ CC12002	Cadzow	Heavy Haulage	£102
❏ CC12003	Nederhoff (dutch)		£35-45
❏ CC12004	Craib Transport		£35-45
❏ CC12005	Pulleyn		£35-45
❏ CC12006	NTM Transport (dutch)		£35-45

Ref.	Model	Range	Price Guide
❏ CC12007	Morris Leslie Ltd	Heavy Haulage	£35-45
❏ CC12008	BJ Waters	Hauliers of Renown	£35-45
❏ CC12009	Lafarge - Estazem	Hauliers of Renown	£35-45
❏ CC12010	Lafarge - Rapidzem	Hauliers of Renown	£35-45
❏ CC12011	Lafarge - Optacolor	Hauliers of Renown	£35-45
❏ CC12012	Phillips of Seahouses Ltd (Ltd Ed 2500)	Hauliers of Renown	£36
❏ CC12013	Matlock Transport Co Ltd	Hauliers of Renown	£35-45

MAN TGA XXL

Ref.	Model	Range	Price Guide
❏ CC13401	Eddie Stobart	Hauliers of Renown	£50-60
❏ CC13403	Ken Thomas Ltd	Hauliers of Renown	£50-60
❏ CC13404	Norman Emerson & Sons Ltd	Hauliers of Renown	£50-60
❏ CC13405	Eddie Stobart	Hauliers of Renown	£50-60

Mercedes Benz Actros

Ref.	Model	Range	Price Guide
❏ CC13801	Eddie Stobart	Hauliers of Renown	£35-45
❏ CC13802	Jack Richards	Truckfest series	£35-45
❏ CC13803	Robert Summers Transport Ltd	Hauliers of Renown	£35-45
❏ CC13804	A Howe & Sons Ltd	Hauliers of Renown	£35-45
❏ CC13805	John Mitchell 50th Anniversary		£35-45
❏ CC13806	Norfolkline	Hauliers of Renown	£37
❏ CC13807	Maurice Hill Transport	Hauliers of Renown	£35-45
❏ CC13808	Yuill & Dodds	Truckfest series	£35-45
❏ CC13809	Pollock	Hauliers of Renown	£35-45
❏ CC13810	Alan Lodge	Truckfest series	£35-45
❏ CC13811	Curran	Hauliers of Renown	£35-45
❏ CC13812	Knauf	Hauliers of Renown	£35-45
❏ CC13813	Rawlings	Hauliers of Renown	£35-45
❏ CC13814	Olivers	Truckfest series	£35-45
❏ CC13815	Pulleyn		£35-45
❏ CC13816	Rawcliffe & Sons Ltd		£35-45
❏ CC13817	Irving Transport	Hauliers of Renown	£35-45

Moffett Kool M5 20.3

Ref.	Model	Range	Price Guide
❏ CC19801	red/black		£5
❏ CC19802	green/black		£5

Renault Van

Ref.	Model	Range	Price Guide
❏ C824	Marcel Gardet		£10
❏ C824/2	Herlouin/Valognes		£10
❏ C824/3	The Lipton		£10
❏ C902	Royal Mail		£65
❏ C917	Courvoisier		£10
❏ C925	Gervais Danone		£10
❏ C823	Jules Goulard		£10
❏ C922	Galeries Lafayette		£10
❏ D889/1	Stella Artois		£10

Renault Premium

Ref.	Model	Range	Price Guide
❏ 75601	Eddie Stobart		£30-40
❏ 75602	Macfarlane		£28
❏ 75603	Norbery		£30-40
❏ 75604	Kent Connection Ltd		£30-40
❏ 75605	Nigel Rice		£30-40
❏ 75606	James Irlam		£30-40
❏ 76101	Damac		£30-40
❏ 76102	Canute		£30-40
❏ CC12102	W Armstrong Ltd		£30-40
❏ CC12103	Feenstra (dutch)		£30-40
❏ CC12104	Strongserve Transport		£30-40
❏ CC12105	Rugby Cement		£30-40
❏ CC12106	Bannerman Transport Ltd	Hauliers of Renown	£30-40

Ref.	Model	Range	Price Guide
❏ CC12107	Dukes Transport	Hauliers of Renown	£23
❏ CC12108	WH Malcolm	Hauliers of Renown	£31
❏ CC12109	RT Keedwell Ltd	Hauliers of Renown	£30-40
❏ CC12111	TNT	Hauliers of Renown	£30-40
❏ CC12112	TTX	Hauliers of Renown	NPA

Scammell Highwayman

Ref.	Model	Range	Price Guide
❏ 16001	Jamesons (Ltd Ed 6500)		£24-28
❏ 16002	Cadbury Bros		£24-28
❏ 16102	Southdown		£24-28
❏ 16201	Pentus Brown		£24-28
❏ 16301	Guinness tanker		£38
❏ 16302	ESSO tanker		£24-28
❏ 16303	Ever Ready tanker		£24-28
❏ 16304	Crow Carrying Co tanker		£24-28
❏ 16305	Tunnel Cement tanker	Building Britain	£24-28
❏ 16306	Shell BP tanker		£24-28
❏ 16401	Siddle Cook		£24-28
❏ 16601	Pickfords	Heavy Haulage	£40
❏ 16701	Wrekin	Heavy Haulage	£24-28
❏ 16702	Pickfords		£24-28
❏ 16703	Pickfords		£24-28
❏ 16704	Pickfords		£24-28
❏ 16801	Pinder (french issue)		£50
❏ 16901	Hallett Silbermann	Heavy Haulage	£24-28
❏ 31010	Short Bros	Heavy Haulage	£45
❏ 97367	Pointer tanker		£24-28
❏ 97368	Pickfords crane		£24-28
❏ 97840	Shell BP tanker		£24-28
❏ 97920	R Edwards		£50
❏ CC10701	BOC		£24-28
❏ CC10702	Mambre & Garton		£24-28
❏ CC10703	Pointer tanker		£24-28
❏ CC10704	Westfield Transport		£24-28
❏ CC10707	Dept of the Environment	Road Transport Heritage	£14

Scammell Constructor

Ref.	Model	Range	Price Guide
❏ 17501	Siddle Cook	Heavy Haulage	£19
❏ 17502	Pickfords wrecker	Heavy Haulage	£28
❏ 17601	Hills of Botley low loader (Ltd Ed 6800)	Heavy Haulage	£44
❏ 17602	Sunter Bros low loader (Ltd Ed 7800)	Heavy Haulage	£46
❏ 17603	Siddle Cook	Heavy Haulage	£50-60
❏ 17701	Pickfords low loader	Heavy Haulage	£50-60
❏ 17702	Wimpey	Building Britain	£50-60
❏ CC11101	Siddle Cook	Heavy Haulage	£30-35
❏ CC11102	Parker Bent	Heavy Haulage	£30-35
❏ CC11103	Pickfords ballast tractor	Road Transport Heritage	£30-35

Scammell Contractor

Ref.	Model	Range	Price Guide
❏ 17901	BRS wrecker truck		£75
❏ 17902	Sunters	Heavy Haulage	£50
❏ 17903	Wynns	Heavy Haulage	£35-40
❏ 17905	Pointer Group	Heavy Haulage	£35-40
❏ 18001	Econofreight with steam turbine load	Heavy Haulage	£55
❏ 18002	Pickfords	Heavy Haulage	£85
❏ 18003	Wynns	Heavy Haulage	£115
❏ 18004	Siddle Cook	Heavy Haulage	£57
❏ 18005	Pickfords with generator load	Heavy Haulage	£135
❏ 18006	Northern Ireland Carriers	Heavy Haulage	£79
❏ 18007	Wrekin Roadways	Heavy Haulage	£92
❏ 31013	ALE	Heavy Haulage	£87
❏ CC12301	United Heavy Transport (Ltd Ed 5000)	Heavy Haulage	£20

Ref.	Model	Range	Price Guide
☐ CC12302	Sunter Brothers	Heavy Haulage	£20-25
☐ CC12303	Austin Brothers Circus	Heavy Haulage	£20-25
☐ CC12304	William Booth & Sons	Heavy Haulage	£20-25
☐ CC12305	Eddie Stobart	Heavy Haulage	£31
☐ CC12306	Eddie Stobart wrecker truck	Heavy Haulage	£19
☐ CC12307	United Heavy Transport girder tailer & load	Heavy Haulage	£49
☐ CC12308	Kaye Goodfellow ballast tractor	Road Transport Heritage	£21

Scammell Crusader
Ref.	Model	Range	Price Guide
☐ CC12002	Eastern BRS		£40-50
☐ CC12601	JR Adams	Kings of the Road	£32
☐ CC12602	CRTS Ackworth Ltd		£40-50
☐ CC12604	Wynns	Heavy Haulage	£40-50
☐ CC12605	Pickfords	Heavy Haulage	£67
☐ CC12607	Eddie Stobart		£40-50
☐ CC12608	BRS		£40-50
☐ CC12609	Morris Young	Hauliers of Renown	£40-50
☐ CC12610	Eddie Stobart low loader		£65

Scammell Scarab
Ref.	Model	Range	Price Guide
☐ 15002	Royal Mail		£15-20
☐ 15003	British Railways		£15-20
☐ 15004	Cadbury		£15-20
☐ 15005	British Railways		£15-20
☐ 15006	Tate & Lyle		£15-20
☐ 15007	Guinness		£15-20
☐ 15101	Express Dairy		£15-20
☐ 15201	M&B		£15-20
☐ 15202	Bulmers (Ltd Ed 5700)		£13
☐ 97318	Websters		£15-20
☐ 97335	Eskimo Frozen Foods		£15-20
☐ 97910	Railfreight		£15-20
☐ 97911	British Railways/Reddings Tea (Ltd Ed 5024)		£23
☐ 97912	Royal Mail		£15-20
☐ 97913	Railfreight, grey		£15-20
☐ 97914	BRS		£15-20
☐ 97916	Corgi Collector Club 10th Anniversary		£15-20
☐ 97917	Watneys		£15-20
☐ CC11301	British Rail		£15-20

Scania 4
Ref.	Model	Range	Price Guide
☐ 76401	Pollock Scotrans curtainside		£39
☐ 76402	Norfolk Line curtainside		£50-60
☐ 76403	Guinness curtainside		£50-60
☐ 76404	Prestons of Potto curtainside		£50-60
☐ 76601	HE Payne refrigerated unit		£50-60
☐ 76603	D Steven refrigerated unit		£50-60
☐ CC12201	Andrew Wishart & Sons Ltd curtainside		£50-60
☐ CC12202	Dukes Transport (Ltd Ed 2900)		£138
☐ CC12203	Eddie Stobart		£50-60
☐ CC12204	Norfolk Line		£50-60
☐ CC12206	Macfarlane Transport		£31
☐ CC12207	Osborne Logistics (Ltd Ed 2800)		£28
☐ CC12208	Van der Weil (dutch)		£50-60
☐ CC12210	WH Malcolm	Heavy Haulage	£50-60
☐ CC12211	Fagan & Walley		£50-60
☐ CC12212	WH Malcolm	Hauliers of Renown	£30-35
☐ CC12213	Westfield Transport curtainside	Hauliers of Renown	£30-35
☐ CC12214	Ken Thomas	Hauliers of Renown	£30-35
☐ CC12215	JR Harding & Sons	Hauliers of Renown	£30-35
☐ CC12217	Marley	Hauliers of Renown	£30-35
☐ CC12218	Ian Craig crane trailer	Hauliers of Renown	£30-35

Ref.	Model	Range	Price Guide
❏ CC12219	Marshalls crane trailer	Hauliers of Renown	£45
❏ CC12220	Gray & Adams		£50
❏ CC12221	British Sugar	Hauliers of Renown	£35-40
❏ CC12222	Olivers Transport Ltd	Hauliers of Renown	£35-40
❏ CC12223	AE Hawkins Ltd	Hauliers of Renown	£35-40
❏ CC12224	Stiller Group tanker	Hauliers of Renown	£35-40

Scania P
❏ CC14201	Rowland Young		£50
❏ CC14202	Tunnocks		£45
❏ CC14203	Yuill & Dodds		£45

Scania R
❏ CC13701	Mason Bros curtainside (Ltd Ed 2254)	Hauliers of Renown	£48
❏ CC13702	Garn Transport	Truckfest	£30
❏ CC13703	CS Ellis	Hauliers of Renown	£50
❏ CC13704	Pollock	Truckfest	£30
❏ CC13705	Scot Trawlers	Hauliers of Renown	£50
❏ CC13706	Knights of Old	Hauliers of Renown	£55
❏ CC13707	SJ Bargh Ltd	Hauliers of Renown	£50-60
❏ CC13708	Lawsons Haulage Ltd	Hauliers of Renown	£50-60
❏ CC13709	CS Ellis	Hauliers of Renown	£50-60
❏ AN13710	Tinnelly Transport 50th Anniversary		£90
❏ CC13711	James Innes	Hauliers of Renown	£50-60
❏ CC13712	Shirleys Transport	Hauliers of Renown	£50-60
❏ CC13713	Prestons of Potto	Hauliers of Renown	£50-60
❏ CC13714	Coles Transport	Truckfest	£32
❏ CC13715	Chris Waite	Hauliers of Renown	£50-60
❏ CC13716	Duncan Hill	Hauliers of Renown	£50-60
❏ CC13717	RG Bassett	Hauliers of Renown	£50-60
❏ CC13718	Johnsons	Hauliers of Renown	£50-60
❏ CC13719	Eddie Stobart	Truckfest	£39
❏ CC13720	Barline Transport	Hauliers of Renown	£50-60

Scania T Cab
❏ CC12801	Ian Hayes bulk tipper (Ltd Ed 5800)		£73
❏ CC12802	Eddie Stobart bulk tipper		£50-60
❏ CC12803	Maguires bulk tipper		£50-60
❏ CC12804	Thomas Heron trailer & crane	Heavy Haulage	£50-60
❏ CC12805	Tinnelly		£50-60
❏ CC12806	JG Riddell		£50-60
❏ CC12807	Cyril Knowles		£39
❏ CC12808	John Toulson	Hauliers of Renown	£50-60
❏ CC12809	Longthorne of Hebdon bulk tipper	Hauliers of Renown	£50-60
❏ CC12810	Sany Kydd trailer & boiler	Heavy Haulage	£50-60
❏ CC12811	Oakfield Haulage curtainside	Hauliers of Renown	£50-60
❏ CC12812	Hadley Group curtainside	Hauliers of Renown	£50-60
❏ CC12813	JJ Bartlett	Hauliers of Renown	£50-60
❏ CC12814	Atchison Topeka Ltd	Hauliers of Renown	£50-60
❏ CC12815	John Toulson tractor unit	Truckfest	£50-60
❏ CC12816	Bulmers Logistics	Hauliers of Renown	£50-60
❏ CC12817	CE Fuller	Truckfest	£50-60
❏ CC12818	G O'Brien & Sons		£50-60
❏ CC12819	GA Smith	Hauliers of Renown	£50-60
❏ CC12820	Coles & Sons (Ltd Ed 2210)	Truckfest	£27

Scania Topline
❏ CC12901	Eddie Stobart curtainside		£35-45
❏ CC12902	Tunderman (dutch)		£35-45
❏ CC12903	Currie European		£35-45
❏ CC12904	D Steven & Son		£43
❏ CC12905	Yull & Dodds		£35-45

Ref.	Model	Range	Price Guide
☐ CC12906	P&C Hamilton		£35-45
☐ CC12907	D Curran & Sons ltd	Hauliers of Renown	£35-45
☐ CC12908	LE Jones Ltd	Hauliers of Renown	£35-45
☐ CC12909	Cadzow tractor unit		£35-45
☐ CC12910	HJ Bentum (dutch)		£35-45
☐ CC12911	Knights of Old	Hauliers of Renown	£35-45
☐ CC12912	Sanderson Ltd	Hauliers of Renown	£35-45
☐ CC12913	TA Jones Ltd	Hauliers of Renown	£35-45
☐ -	Corby Chilled Distribution		£48
☐ CC12916	Montgomery Transport	Hauliers of Renown	£35-45
☐ CC12917	Henry Thomson & Sons	Hauliers of Renown	£35-45
☐ CC12918	Pentons	Hauliers of Renown	£35-45
☐ CC12919	MacTaggart Bros livestock transporter	Hauliers of Renown	£35-45
☐ CC12920	AL Campbell (Ltd Ed 3000)	Hauliers of Renown	£61
☐ CC12921	Kenneth McWilliam bulk tipper	Hauliers of Renown	£35-45
☐ CC12922	Trevor Pye Transport	Hauliers of Renown	£35-45
☐ CC12923	Macfarlane Transport Ltd	Truckfest	£35-45
☐ CC12925	Baggeridge Brick		£35-45
☐ CC12926	Mulgrew curtainside	Hauliers of Renown	£35-45
☐ CC12927	Archers Transport curtainside	Hauliers of Renown	£35-45
☐ CC12928	RW Stewart (Ltd Ed 2010)	Hauliers of Renown	£83
☐ CC12929	Dennis Oates	Hauliers of Renown	£35-45
☐ CC12930	RS Carmichael/Joey Dunlop	Hauliers of Renown	£99
☐ CC12931	Pollock (Ltd Ed 1510)	Sights and Sounds	£52
☐ CC12933	Edward Gilder & Co	Hauliers of Renown	£35-45
☐ CC12934	J Anderson Transport	Hauliers of Renown	£35-45
☐ CC12935	Ian Hayes Transport	Sights and Sounds	£75
☐ CC12936	Eddie Stobart	Sights and Sounds	£85
☐ CC12937	Olivers	Sights and Sounds	£85

Thorneycroft Van

Ref.	Model		Price Guide
☐ C820	East Anglian Fruit Co		
☐ C821	Castrol		£8-10
☐ C821/1	Heidelberger Druckautomat		£8-10
☐ C827	GWR		£8-10
☐ C828	Gamleys		£8-10
☐ C830	Jacobs		£8-10
☐ C831	Huntley & Palmers		£8-10
☐ C832	Corgi 1st Anniversary - Fforestfach Ind Est		£8-10
☐ C832	Corgi 1st Anniversary - Swansea Ind Est		£8-10
☐ C833	McFarlane Lane		£8-10
☐ C834	Lyons		£8-10
☐ C836	LMS		£8-10
☐ C837	SR		£8-10
☐ C838	LNER		£8-10
☐ C839	Nurdin & Peacock		£8-10
☐ C840	Allenburys Foods		£8-10
☐ C841	Peek Freans		£8-10
☐ C842	Carter Paterson/Scweppes		£8-10
☐ C843	Eddershaws		£8-10
☐ C845	Duckhams		£8-10
☐ C846	Ind Coope/Alsops		£8-10
☐ C847	James Keiller		£8-10
☐ C848	News of the World		£8-10
☐ C853	MA Rapport		£8-10
☐ C854	Lincolnshire Ambulance		£8-10
☐ C855	Lincolnshire Fire		£8-10
☐ C856	Lincolnshire Police		£8-10
☐ C859	Thorleys Cattle Food		£8-10
☐ C859/1	Scotts Empire Bread		£8-10
☐ C859/2	Chivers Jam		£8-10
☐ C859/3	Arnotts Biscuits		£8-10

Ref.	Model	Range	Price Guide
❑ C859/4	Goodyear		£8-10
❑ C859/5	Grattons		£8-10
❑ C859/7	Leda Salts		£8-10
❑ C859/8	Volvolutum Soap		£8-10
❑ C859/9	ASDA, blue version		£8-10
❑ C859/10	Batchelors		£8-10
❑ C859/11	Lea & Perrins		£8-10
❑ C859/13	McDougalls		£8-10
❑ C859/16	ASDA - 25th Anniversary silver version		£8-10
❑ C867	Thomas Wethered beer lorry		£8-10
❑ C867/1	Charlese Wells beer lorry		£8-10
❑ C867/2	Tooheys Pilsner beer lorry		£8-10
❑ C867/3	Swan Brewery beer lorry		£8-10
❑ C867/4	Carlsberg beer lorry		£8-10
❑ C882	St Winifreds beer lorry		£8-10
❑ C883	Taunton Cider beer lorry		£8-10
❑ C907	HP Sauce		£8-10
❑ C910	Small & Parkes		£8-10
❑ C911	Persil		£8-10
❑ C913	Dewars		£8-10
❑ C914	Liptons Tea		£8-10
❑ C915	OXO		£8-10
❑ C923	Red Cross ambulance		£8-10
❑ C923/2	Troesch (swiss)		£57
❑ C924	Safeway		£8-10
❑ C926	Double Diamond		£8-10
❑ C929	Gamleys		£8-10
❑ C931	Stepney Tyres		£8-10
❑ C932	Puritan Soap		£8-10
❑ C933	Punch		£8-10
❑ C968	Radio Steiner		£15-20
❑ 9001	Fry's		£8-10
❑ 96970	Boots		£10-12
❑ 97150	Buckingham Palace	Royalty	£15-20
❑ 97151	Sandringham	Royalty	£15-20
❑ 97152	Windsor Castle	Royalty	£15-20
❑ 97153	Holyrood House	Royalty	£15-20
❑ 97154	Kensington Palace	Royalty	£15-20
❑ 97155	Balmoral	Royalty	£15-20
❑ CC09001	Corgi Club 21st Birthday, red roof		NPA
❑ CC09001	Corgi Club 21st Birthday, white roof		£12-15

Volvo F88

Ref.	Model	Range	Price Guide
❑ CC13101	Eddie Stobart box trailer	Hauliers of Renown	£33
❑ CC13102	William Nicol Ltd log trailer	Hauliers of Renown	£40-50
❑ CC13103	Elddis Transport Tautliner	Hauliers of Renown	£40-50
❑ CC13104	Hoveringham low loader	Heavy Haulage	£40-50
❑ CC13105	BRS		£40-50
❑ CC13106	HE Payne	Hauliers of Renown	£40-50
❑ CC13107	Pollock	Hauliers of Renown	£40-50
❑ CC13108	Mansel Davies & Sons Ltd	Hauliers of Renown	£40-50
❑ CC13109	Andrew Wishart & Sons ltd	Hauliers of Renown	£40-50
❑ CC13110	Heanor Haulage low loader	Heavy Haulage	£40-50
❑ CC13111	David McCulla & Sons		£40-50

Volvo FH

Ref.	Model	Range	Price Guide
❑ AN14001	Mancel Davies 50th Anniversary	Hauliers of Renown	£79
❑ CC14002	Eddie Stobart	Hauliers of Renown	£45-50
❑ CC14003	Reid Transport	Hauliers of Renown	£45-50
❑ CC14004	JG McWilliam	Truckfest	£34
❑ CC14005	Benton Bros	Hauliers of Renown	£45-50
❑ CC14006	Intake Transport	Hauliers of Renown	£45-50

Ref.	Model	Range	Price Guide
❑ CC14007	East West with Volvo excavator		£45-50
❑ CC14008	Highland Haulage	Hauliers of Renown	£45-50
❑ CC14009	Rowland	Hauliers of Renown	£45-50
❑ CC14010	Smith Anderson	Hauliers of Renown	£45-50
❑ CC14011	Hockin	Hauliers of Renown	£29
❑ CC14012	Stobart with box trailer	Hauliers of Renown	£45-50

Volvo FH Globetrotter

Ref.	Model	Range	Price Guide
❑ CC12401	Eddie Stobart curtainside		£45-50
❑ CC12402	Owens Road Services Ltd curtainside		£45-50
❑ CC12403	Heanor	Heavy Haulage	£70
❑ CC12404	Chris Bennett	Heavy Haulage	£45-50
❑ CC12405	Eddie Stobart tractor		£45-50
❑ CC12406	Banks Bros low loader	Heavy Haulage	£45-50
❑ CC12407	Van der Linden (dutch) curtainside		£45-50
❑ CC12408	Doorenbos Transport (dutch) curtainside (Ltd Ed 2600)		£33
❑ CC12409	McBurney fridge trailer		£45-50
❑ CC12410	Knowles Transport bulk tipper		£45-50
❑ CC12412	E Nuttall	Heavy Haulage	£45-50
❑ CC12413	Van de Wetering (dutch) low loader & boat		£75
❑ CC12414	Alex Anderson sawdust trailer		£45-50
❑ CC12415	P Hincliffe bulk tipper		£45-50
❑ CC12416	Jefferies of Otley curtainside (Ltd Ed 2600)	Hauliers of Renown	£26
❑ CC12417	A Wishart & Sons Ltd tractor unit	Hauliers of Renown	£17
❑ CC12418	Harry Lawson Ltd curtainside	Hauliers of Renown	£45-50
❑ CC12419	Van der Kwaak (dutch) fridge trailer	Hauliers of Renown	£45-50
❑ CC12420	Scotlee fridge trailer	Hauliers of Renown	£45-50
❑ CC12421	Lomas Distribution tanker	Hauliers of Renown	£45-50
❑ CC12422	John Somerscales Ltd	Heavy Haulage	£45-50
❑ CC12424	LE Jones livestock transporter	Hauliers of Renown	£45-50
❑ CC12426	Douglas F Mitchell Ltd bulk tipper	Hauliers of Renown	£45-50
❑ CC12427	Inta Site Haulage crane trailer	Hauliers of Renown	£45-50
❑ CC12428	Fred Greenwood livestock transporter	Hauliers of Renown	£45-50
❑ CC12429	Cooper Buckley Ltd tipper	Hauliers of Renown	£33
❑ CC12430	NT Whitfield Transport Ltd (Ltd Ed 1760)	Hauliers of Renown	£36

Volvo FM

Ref.	Model	Range	Price Guide
❑ CC13501	Davidson Bros tipper		£45-50
❑ CC13502	Tarmac tipper		£45-50
❑ CC13503	Rugby RMC curtainside	Hauliers of Renown	£45-50
❑ CC13504	WH Malcolm tipper		£45-50
❑ CC13505	Ed Weetman bulk tipper	Hauliers of Renown	£45-50
❑ CC13506	E Pawson & Sons Ltd box trailer	Hauliers of Renown	£45-50
❑ CC13507	RF Fieilding curtainside	Hauliers of Renown	£45-50
❑ CC13508	Yuill & Dodds		£45-50
❑ CC13509	JW Morrison tipper		£45-50
❑ CC13510	James Booth bulk tipper	Hauliers of Renown	£45-50
❑ CC13511	Lafarge tipper		£45-50
❑ CC13512	Ian Craig curtainside (Ltd Ed 1870)	Hauliers of Renown	£37
❑ CC13513	Pridmores Haulage tipper		£45-50
❑ CC13514	Albert Fyfe bulk tipper		£45-50
❑ CC13515	The Real McKay Ltd		£45-50
❑ CC13516	Countrywide Farmers		£45-50
❑ CC13517	N Irving Transport		£45-50
❑ CC13518	Cemex	Hauliers of Renown	£45-50
❑ CC13520	DR Macleod		£29
❑ CC13521	Highland Haulage (Ltd Ed 1160)		£35
❑ CC13522	Knights of Old		£29
❑ CC13523	MM & LM Finnie	Truckfest	£45-50
❑ CC13524	Skye Transport	Hauliers of Renown	£78

Volvo (1:64 Scale)

Ref.	Model	Range	Price Guide
❑ 98100	Swift		£8-10

Ref.	Model	Range	Price Guide
☐ 98101	Amtrak		£8-10
☐ 98102	UTC		£8-10
☐ 98103	P&O		£8-10
☐ 98104	Christian Salvesen		£8-10
☐ 98105	Exel		£8-10
☐ 98106	Dodd's Transport		£8-10
☐ 98107	Lynx		£8-10
☐ 59529	ERF - Guinness		£10-12
☐ 59530	Volvo - Guinness		£10-12
☐ 59531	Scania - Guinness		£10-12
☐ 59557	Renault - Cavewood		£10-12
☐ 59558	Scannia - PHH Distribution		£10-12
☐ 59559	ERF - CS Ellis		£10-12
☐ 59562	Volvo Christian Salvesen		£10-12
☐ 59563	Renault & Leyland Comet 2pce set - Guinness		£21
☐ 59564	Scania & Karrier Dropside 2pce set - Guinness		£23
☐ 59565	Volvo & Commer 2pce set - Guinness		£10-12
☐ CC86601	Scania - gold plated Eddie Stobart		£24
☐ CC86603	Scania - Sunpride		£10-12
☐ CC86604	Scania - Knauf		£10-12
☐ CC86612	Scania - 2002 Manchester Commonwealth Games		£10-12
☐ CC86701	Volvo - United Glass		£10-12
☐ CP86734	Volvo - Superior Fires		£10-12
☐ CC86702	Volvo - The Mirror		£10-12
☐ CP86910	Renault - RF Freight		£10-12
☐ CC87003	Leyland Daf - James Irlam		£10-12

TRAILERS (individually packaged units)

Ref.	Model	Range	Price Guide
☐ CC19901	blue curtainside (no livery)		NPA
☐ CC19902	Gibbs of Fraserburgh		£42
☐ CC19903	HE Payne curtainside		£19
☐ CC19904	Eddie Stobart curtainside		£19
☐ CC19905	Pollock curtainside		£19
☐ 75407R	Guinness		£14-18

1:76 SCALE
Mercedes Benz Aactros

Ref.	Model	Range	Price Guide
☐ CC18201	Charles GEE & CO Ltd	Roadscene	£15-20
☐ CC18202	Phillips of Seahouse Ltd	Roadscene	£15-20
☐ CC18203	John Mitchell	Roadscene	£15-20
☐ CC18204	Camden Group	Roadscene	£15-20

Scania R

Ref.	Model	Range	Price Guide
☐ CC18101	Tyneside Express	Roadscene	£15-20
☐ CC18102	Scott Trawlers	Roadscene	£15-20
☐ CC18103	JBT	Roadscene	£15-20
☐ CC18104	Hadfields	Roadscene	£15-20

Volvo FH

Ref.	Model	Range	Price Guide
☐ CC18001	Pollock	Roadscene	£15-20
☐ CC18002	Whitelink Seafoods	Roadscene	£15-20
☐ CC18003	Mansell Davies & Sons	Roadscene	£15-20
☐ CC18004	Eddie Stobart	Roadscene	£15-20

Gift Sets

Ref.	Model	Range	Price Guide
☐ D7/1	Royal Mail 2pce		£10-15
☐ D9/1	Shell 2pce		£10-15
☐ D15	GPO Telephones 2pce		£10-15
☐ D17/1	Shell 2pce		£10-15
☐ D23/1	Ford Popular 3pce		£10-15
☐ D35/1	Battle of Britain 3pce 50th Anniversary		£10-15
☐ D46/1	British Railways Morris J & Bedford S 2pce set (Ltd Ed 13000)		£14

Ref.	Model		Price Guide
❑ C49	Times 2pce		£10-15
❑ C50	Billingsgate, Covent garden & Smithfield Markets 3pce		£10-15
❑ D51/1	Green King 2pce Brewery set		£10-15
❑ D52/1	Charringtons 2pce Brewery set		£10-15
❑ D54/1	National Resources 4pce		£10-15
❑ Q55/1	York Fair 2pce 225th Anniversary		£10-15
❑ Q57/1	Northern Collection 2pce		£10-15
❑ D67/1	United Dairies 2pce		£10-15
❑ C68	Kays 2pce		£10-15
❑ C69	Englands Glory 2pce		£10-15
❑ D71/1	Ford Model T 4pce		£10-15
❑ D72/1	Morris Minor & Ford Popular Vans 4pce		£10-15
❑ D74/1	Pickfords 3pce set		£19
❑ D82/1	Corgi We're On the Move 2pce		£20-25
❑ C88	Military Vans 2pce (Ltd Ed 7500)		£10-15
❑ C90	Ford Utility 2pce		£10-15
❑ C91	Morris Minor Vans 3pce		£15-20
❑ D94/1	Whitbread 2pce Brewery set		£8
❑ 8002	Royal Mail 2pce		£10-15
❑ 8007	Cadbury's 2pce		£10-15
❑ 8008	Guinness 2pce		£10-15
❑ 31002	National Benzole 2pce		£27
❑ 31004	Wynns 2pce	Heavy Haulage	£39
❑ 31005	Shell BP 2pce (Ltd Ed 5500)		£27
❑ 31006	Wynns 2pce (Ltd Ed 6600)	Heavy Haulage	£29
❑ 31008	Wimpey 2pce		£42
❑ 31009	Wynns 2pce		£49
❑ 31701	Eddie Stobart 2pce		£32
❑ 31704	Eddie Stobart 2pce		£34
❑ 76901	Eddie Stobart 5pce tractor unit (plinth mounted)		£97
❑ 96995	Ian Allan 50th Anniversary (Ltd Ed 6000)		£10-15
❑ 97200	BRS Parcels 2pce		£15-20
❑ 97714	D-Day 4pce		£29
❑ 97735	Cumbrian 3pce		£15-20
❑ 97740	The Times 2pce set		£10
❑ 97742	John Smiths 2pce Brewery set		£10-15
❑ 97746	Toymaster 2pce		£10-15
❑ 97747	Websters 2pce Brewery set		£10-15
❑ 97749	British Railways Popular & Bedford 2pce set (Ltd Ed 5000)		£14
❑ 97751	Bass 2pce Brewery set		£10-15
❑ 97752	Ruddles Brewery 2pce set		£10-15
❑ 97753	Terry's Chocolate 2pce		£10-15
❑ 97754	LMS 2pce		£10-15
❑ 97755	Whitbread 25th Anniversary 2pce Brewery set		£10-15
❑ 97765	Strathblair 2pce		£10-15
❑ 97781	Tate & Lyle 2pce		£17
❑ -	Royal Mail 3pce		£10
❑ CC99125	Gibbs 'End of the Road' 3pce		£241
❑ CC99129	Norfolk Line 3pce		£47
❑ CC99130	Pollock 4pce (Ltd Ed 2700)		£180
❑ CC99131	Harris & Minors 'Final Chapter' 2pce (Ltd Ed 3400)		£48
❑ CC99140	The Scammell Story 6pce tractor unit set		£89
❑ CC99147	HE Payne 4pce set		£98
❑ CC99154	Moreton C Cullimore 2pce		£96
❑ CC99155	Scania Stobart 3pce		£88
❑ CC99164	Pride of the Dales 3pce		£93
❑ CC99165	Lord of the Isles 4pce		£65-75
❑ CC99169	Barry Proctor 2pce		£65-75
❑ CC99173	Benton Bros 4pce		£65-75
❑ CC99174	WH Malcolm 4pce		£65-75
❑ CC99185	150 Years of Foden 3pce		£117
❑ CC99188	Stan Robinson 4pce		NPA
❑ CC99192	David Haig 4pce		£65-750

VANS

1:50 SCALE

❑ CC14301	JCB Construction Ford Transit		£14
❑ CC14401	BT Vauxhall Vivero		£15-20
❑ CC14501	AA Renault Trafic		£15-20

Bedford CA (1:43)

❑ D981/1	Pickfords		£5-9
❑ D981/2	Cambrian News		£5-9
❑ D981/3	AA (renumbered 96903, 99805 & 98105)		£5-9
❑ D981/4	Express Dairies		£5-9
❑ D981/7	Corgi Collectors Club		£5-9
❑ D981/9	Evening News		£5-9
❑ D981/10	Evening Standard		£5-9
❑ D981/11	The Star		£5-9
❑ D981/12	Gas		£5-9
❑ 5601	Kodak	Golden Oldies	£5-9
❑ 5602	Ovaltine, blue	Golden Oldies	£5-9
❑ 5603	KLG Plugs, red	Archive Corgi	£5-9
❑ 5604	AFS Personnel Carrier (see Emergency)		£5-9
❑ 5605	Royal Mail		£5-9
❑ 5606	Beatles Collection, graffiti		£10-13
❑ 5607	RAC		£5-9
❑ 96900	Manchester Evening News		£5-9
❑ 96904	RAC		£5-9
❑ CC02601	Corgi Toys		£5-9

Bedford Dormobile 1:43

❑ D982/1	cream/blue		£5-9
❑ D982/2	red/cream		£5-9
❑ D982/3	green/cream		£5-9
❑ D982/4	brown/cream		£5-9
❑ 96920	Police, dk blue (renumbered 99806)		£5-9
❑ 96923	St Johns Ambulance		£5-9

Ford Model T van 1:43

❑ C865	Lyons, black roof		£37
❑ C865	Lyons, white roof		£5-9
❑ C865/1	Needlers		£5-9
❑ C865/2	Drummers Dyes		£5-9
❑ C865/3	Kalamanzoo		£5-9
❑ C865/4	Pepsi		£5-9
❑ C865/5	Twinnings		£5-9
❑ C865/7	Kays		£5-9
❑ C865/11	Steiff		£5-9
❑ C865/14	NAAFI		£16
❑ C865/15	John Menzies		£5-9
❑ C873	Zebra Polish		£5-9
❑ C874	Corgi Collectors Club		£5-9
❑ C875	Stollwerk Schokolade		£5-9
❑ C876	Dickens & Jones		£5-9
❑ C877	Royal Mail		£5-9
❑ C965	Ford 75th Anniversary, yellow lettering		£5-9
❑ C966	Ford 75th Anniversary, white lettering, gold or white window		£5-9
❑ 8101	Cadbury Bournville Cocoa		£5-9
❑ 97469	Victrola		£5-9

Ford Model T tanker 1:43

❑ C864	Pratts		£5-7
❑ C864/1	Staileys		£5-7
❑ C864/2	Rimmers		£5-7
❑ C864/3	San Francisco Fire Dept		£5-7

☐ C864/4	Nationale Benzole		£5-7
☐ C864/6	Olympic Gasoline		£5-7
☐ C872	Dominion		£5-7
☐ C880	BP		£5-7

Ford Popular van 1:43

☐ D980/1	SA Peacock		£5-9
☐ D980/2	Fullers Radio & Television		£5-9
☐ D980/3	Luton Motor Co		£8-10
☐ D980/4	Corgi Collector Club		£8-10
☐ D980/8	Pearsons Carpets		£8-10
☐ D980/12	Sheldon Light Haulage		£8-10
☐ D980/13	Lima Furniture		£8-10
☐ D980/14	Cambrian Factory Ltd		£8-10
☐ D980/15	Abbey Colour		£8-10
☐ D980/16	Royal Mail (renumbered 98108)		£8-10
☐ 5901	Royal Mail		£8-10
☐ 96860	Eastbourne Motors		£8-10
☐ 96863	Sunlight Soap		£8-10
☐ 96866	Gas		£8-10

Ford Transit 1:43

☐ CC07801	WH Malcolm		£5-8
☐ CC07802	Stan Robinson		£5-8
☐ CC07803	DR Macleod		£5-8
☐ CC07804	MacFarlane		£5-8
☐ CC07805	British Gas		£5-8
☐ CC07806	McCulla		£5-8
☐ CC07807	Eddie Stobart		£5-8
☐ CC07808	BT		£5-8
☐ CC07809	Ian Hayes		£5-8
☐ CC07810	Scott Trawlers		£5-8

Land Rover 1:43

☐ 7101	1996 Corgi Club model		£8-10
☐ 7102	Mersey Tunnel breakdown truck		£8-10
☐ 7103	Gold plated		£13
☐ 7105	Silver plated		£17
☐ 301	Home Office		£8-10
☐ 7302	British Army		£8-10
☐ 7401	Royal Mail		£8-10
☐ 7402	Eddie Stobart		£8-10
☐ 7403	AA		£8-10
☐ 7404	Maidstone & District		£8-10
☐ 7406	Coastguard		£8-10
☐ 7407	Bath Fire Brigade		£8-10
☐ 7408	BOAC		£8-10
☐ 7414	RAC		£8-10
☐ 7502	Tarmac 2pce set with trailer (Ltd Ed 2000)	Building Britain	£42
☐ CC07404	Mud slashed green version		£8-10
☐ CC07405	Rover Mobile Service		£8-10
☐ CC07406	RAC		£8-10

Land Rover 110 Defender 1:43

☐ CC07701	Coniston		£8-10
☐ CC07703	AA		£8-10
☐ CC07705	County Station Wagon		£8-10
☐ CC07706	Eddie Stobart		£8-10
☐ CC07708	Royal Mail		£8-10
☐ CC07713	Yorkshire Rider		£8-10

Morris J van 1:43

	Ref.	Model		Price
❏	D983/1	PO Telephones		£5-8
❏	D983/2	Royal Mail (renumbered 96893)		£5-8
❏	D983/3	Corgi Collectors Club		£5-8
❏	D983/4	Metropolitan Police		£5-8
❏	D983/5	Walls Ice Cream (renumbered 98101)		£5-8
❏	96880	Pickfords (renumbered 99802)		£5-8
❏	6201	Cydrax	Golden Oldies	£5-8
❏	6202	Oxo	Golden Oldies	£5-8
❏	6203	Royal Mail		£5-8
❏	6204	RAC		£5-8
❏	6891	Morris Service		£5-8
❏	-	Royal Worcester		£5-8
❏	96886	Family Assusance Friendly Soc.		£5-8
❏	96888	Southdown		£5-8
❏	96892	Bovril		£5-8
❏	96893	Royal Mail		£5-8
❏	96894	Post Office		£5-8
❏	96895	Birmingham Transport (General Manager)		£5-8
❏	96895	Birmingham Transport (Genetal Manager spelling error)		£12

Morris Minor van 1:43

	Ref.	Model		Price
❏	C957/1	Royal Mail, metal base (UK) & plastic base (Portugal)		£14
❏	C957/2	Gas		£5-8
❏	C957/3	Corgi Collectors Club		£5-8
❏	C957/4	Castrol		£5-8
❏	C957/5	Michelin		£5-8
❏	C957/6	Foyles		£5-8
❏	C957/7	MacFisheries		£5-8
❏	C957/11	Appleyard Nuffield		£5-8
❏	D957/12	D Morgan		£5-8
❏	D957/13	Kimberley Clark		£5-8
❏	Q957/20	Guernsey PO		£5-8
❏	D957/21	7 UP		£5-8
❏	C958/1	Post Office, metal base (UK) & plastic base (Portugal)		£11
❏	Q957/24	BATR		£23
❏	Q957/26	NAMAC		£5-8
❏	C959	Smiths Crisps		£5-8
❏	6501	Shell BP	Golden Oldies	£5-8
❏	6502	Nestles	Golden Oldies	£5-8
❏	6503	Royal Mail		£5-8
❏	6504	TV License Investigation		£5-8
❏	6505	British Caledonian Airways		£5-8
❏	6506	Courtline		£5-8
❏	6507	BRS		£16
❏	6508	RAC		£5-8
❏	-	Royal Worcester		£5-8
❏	96837	Maidstone & Dist.		£5-8
❏	96839	Royal Mail		£5-8
❏	96840	Bristol Water		£5-8
❏	96842	PO Telephones, yellow (renumbered 99803)		£5-8
❏	96843	NAMAC		£5-8
❏	96844	A Dunn & Son		£5-8
❏	96845	Bishops Removals		£5-8
❏	96847	Colmans Mustard		£5-8
❏	96848	Birds Custard		£5-8
❏	96849	AA		£5-8
❏	96852	Gaydon 3rd Motor Show		£5-8
❏	97541	PO Engineering		£5-8
❏	98104	Royal Mail		£5-8
❏	-	Royal Mail Driver Training		£5-8

Ref.	Model	Range	Price Guide
Morris Minor Pick Up 1:43			
❑ 6301	Dan Air		£5-8
❑ 96850	Wimpey		£5-8
❑ 96851	LBC		£5-8
❑ 97344	Blue Circle Cement		£5-8
❑ 97344	Tarmac		£5-8
Morris Minor Traveller 1:43			
❑ 97343	Bomb Disposal		£5-8
❑ -	Corgi Collector Club		£5-8
Mini van 1:43			
❑ 6001	PO Telephones		£5-8
❑ 6003	BKS		£5-8
❑ 6004	RAC		£5-8
❑ 96950	Royal Mail		£5-8
❑ 96952	RAC Radio Service		£5-8
❑ 96953	AA		£5-8
❑ 96955	1994 Corgi Collector Club		£10
❑ 97337	Fawley Refinery Fire van		£5-8
❑ 97770	Hamleys		£5-8
❑ 97771	Cavendish Woodhouse		£5-8
❑ 97772	Burberrys		£5-8
❑ -	Royal Mail		£5-8
Reliant Van			
❑ CC85801	Eddie Stobart (1:36)		£9
❑ -	Royal Mail Supervan MkIII (1:43 scale)		£5-8
VW van 1:43			
❑ D985/1	blue		£5-8
❑ 6901	red/cream		£5-8
❑ 6902	Lowenbrau	German Series	£5-8
❑ 6903	Berliner Kindl	German Series	£5-8
❑ 6904	Holsten	German Series	£5-8
❑ 7001	Luftansa		£5-8
❑ 96960	Bosch		£5-8
❑ 96965	1992 Corgi Collector Club		£5-8
VW Camper van 1:43			
❑ D984/1	red/grey		£5-8
❑ 6801	cream/green		£5-8
❑ 96941	grey/white		£5-8
❑ 97040	green/white		£5-8

BUS, COACH, TRAM & TAXI

AEC Q Type Double Decker Bus

❑	OM45701	London Transport - route 77	£12
❑	OM45702	Bradford City	£12
❑	OM45703	London Transport - Private Hire. Model Collector 2500 Ltd Ed.	£16
❑	OM45704	London Transport - Country Area (Fishpools label)	£11
❑	OM45705	Westcliff	£10-12
❑	OM45706	Kingston	£10-12
❑	OM45707	Cardiff	£10-12
❑	OM45708	Leeds	£10-12
❑	OM45709	Bolton	£10-12
❑	OM45710	Halifax	£10-12
❑	OM45711	Birmingham - route 1A	£10-12
❑	OM45711	Birmingham - route 16	£15

AEC Q Type Single Deck

❑	OM41001	London Transport (1934) - route 312	£10-12
❑	OM41002	London Transport (wartime) - route 434	£10-12
❑	OM41003	London Transport (Central) - route 218, open door	£10-12
❑	OM41004	London Transport (Central) - route 218, closed door	£10-12
❑	OM41005	Green Line	£10-12
❑	OM41006	Malta	£10-12
❑	OM41007	London Transport - route 497, green	£10-12
❑	OM41008	London Transport - route 215	£10-12
❑	OM41009	London Transport - no route, green	£10-12
❑	OM41010	London Transport - Civil Defence	£10-12

AEC Regent II (Weymann)

❑	40401	Kingston	£10-12
❑	40402	Newcastle	£10-12
❑	40403	Eastbourne	£10-12
❑	40404	Brighton - route 52	£10-12
❑	40405	Grimsby	£10-12
❑	40406	Oxford - maroon roof	£10-12
❑	40406	Oxford - red roof	£10-12
❑	40409	Aberdeen	£10-12
❑	40410	Widnes	£10-12
❑	40411	Morecombe & Heysham	£10-12
❑	97814	London Transport - route 321 (Ltd ed 11000)	£10-12
❑	OM40401	South Wales	£10-12
❑	OM40402	Brighton - route 26	£10-12
❑	OM40403	London Transport - route 351	£10-12

AEC Regent V (Orion)

❑	41001	Aberdeen	£10-12
❑	41002	Hebble	£10-12
❑	41003	Devon	£10-12
❑	97943	Douglas	£10-12

AEC Reliance

❑	40202	BEA	£10-12
❑	97130	Oxford	£10-12
❑	97900	Devon	£10-12
❑	97902	PMT	£10-12
❑	97904	Leicester	£10-12
❑	OM40203	Aldershot	£10-12
❑	41501	AEC Breakdown Lorry, MacBraynes	£10-12

AEC Tower Wagon

❑	42101	Brighton	£13
❑	42102	London Transport - grey	£18
❑	42103	London Transport - red	£12

AEC Regent Utility

☐	43904	Leicester - Rapid advert	£9
☐	43911	Leicester - CWS advert	£18
☐	43915	Edinburgh	£11

Bedford OB Coach (quarterlights)

☐	42501	Royal Blue	£23
☐	42502	Trossachs Trundler	£10-12
☐	42503	Hants & Dorset	£10-12
☐	42504	Crosville	£10-12
☐	42505	Malta	£10-12
☐	42506	Loch Tay Trundler	£10-12

Bedford OB Coach (no quarterlights)

☐	42601	MacBraynes	£16
☐	42602	Mountain Goat	£10-12
☐	42603	Hants & Sussex	£17
☐	42604	Grey-Green	£10-12
☐	42605	Seagull Coaches	£10-12
☐	42606	Guinness	£10-12
☐	42607	Southdown	£10-12
☐	42608	Yelloways	£10-12
☐	42609	British Railways	£10-12
☐	42610	Alexander & Sons	£10-12
☐	42611	Edinburgh	£10-12
☐	42612	Alexander & Sons	£16
☐	OM42601	Malta	£10-12
☐	OM42602	Bibby's of Ingleton	£10-12
☐	CP42603	Aland Post	£10-12
☐	CP42604	Kenzies	£10-12
☐	CP42605	Finland Post Office	£10-12

Blackpool Balloon Tram

☐	43501	1960s livery - Cabin destination	£26
☐	43502	Wartime livery	£12-15
☐	43503	Pre-war livery	£12-15
☐	43504	Blackpool Illuminations	£12-15
☐	43505	1960s livery - Pleasure Beach destination	£12-15
☐	43506	1934 livery	£12-15
☐	43507	Empire Pools	£12-15
☐	43508	Walls Ice Cream - Pleasure Beach destination	£12-15
☐	43509	1990s livery	£12-15
☐	43510	1934 livery (1994 2nd version)	£12-15
☐	43511	1990s livery (2nd version)	£12-15
☐	43512	Pontins	£12-15
☐	43513	1980s livery	£12-15
☐	43514	Blackpool Pleasure Beach	£12-15
☐	43515	Michelin (motorised)	£28
☐	43516	Goosebumps	£12-15
☐	OM43501	Thwaites	£12-15
☐	OM43502	Valhalla	£12-15
☐	OM43503	Blackpool Lights	£12-15
☐	OM43504	Eclipse	£12-15
☐	OM43505	Walls Ice Cream - Tower destination	£12-15
☐	OM43506	1980s livery	£17
☐	OM43507	1950s livery	£21
☐	OM43508	1960s livery - Milady advert	£15-20
☐	OM43509	Eclipse	£15-20
☐	OM43510	Mystique - Bispham destination	£19
☐	OM43510	Mystique - Cabin destination	£18
☐	OM43511	Hot Ice - Cabin destination	£12-15
☐	OM43511	Hot Ice - Pleasure Beach destination	£12-15

Blackpool Brush Railcoach

	Ref.	Model	Price
❏	44001	Original livery	£9
❏	44002	Current livery	£8
❏	44004	Blackpool Zoo	£12
❏	44005	Wartime livery	£13
❏	44006	Hot Ice	£11
❏	OM44001	British Legion Poppy Appeal	£50
❏	OM44002	Terror Train	£17
❏	OM44003	Sandcastle	£19
❏	OM44004	Mystique	£13
❏	OM44005	1960s livery	£14
❏	OM44006	Royal Mail	£11
❏	OM44007	Brannigans	£11
❏	OM44008	Sealife Centre	£11
❏	OM44009	Laughing Donkey	£11
❏	OM44010	Metro Coastlines	£11
❏	OM44011	Fleetwood Market - Fleetwood destination	£14
❏	OM44011	Fleetwood Market - Starr Gate destination	£14
❏	OM44012	Tigeriffic - Bispham destination	£17
❏	OM44012	Tigeriffic - Starr Gate destination	£17

Bova Futura

	Ref.	Model	Price
❏	45301	Wiltshire & Dorset National Express	£10-12
❏	43502	Johnsons	£10-12
❏	41703	Flights	£10-12
❏	39904	Forestdale	£10-12
❏	OM45301	Paul Winson	£10-12
❏	OM45302	Eurolines	£10-12
❏	OM45303	Anderson Travel	£10-12
❏	OM45304	Woods	£10-12
❏	OM45305	Bruces National Express	£10-12
❏	OM45306	Durham City	£10-12
❏	OM45307	Kings Ferry	£10-12
❏	OM45308	National Express	£16
❏	OM45309	Maynes	£14
❏	OM45310	Kings Tours	£10-12

BMMO C5 Coach

	Ref.	Model	Price
❏	OM45501	Midland Red - Motorway Coach, London destination	£13-16
❏	OM45502	Lichfield Speedway	£13-16
❏	OM45503	Midland Red - Llandudno destination	£13-16
❏	OM45504	Midland Red - Birmingham destination	£13-16
❏	OM45505	Midland - Tamworth destination	£13-16
❏	OM45506	Midland Red - Motorway Express, London destination	£19
❏	OM45507	Midland Red - OOC Club model	£13-16

BMMO D9 Bus

	Ref.	Model	Price
❏	OM45601	Midland Red - route 154	£13-16
❏	OM45602	London Transport Sightseeing Tour (open top)	£13-16
❏	OM45603	West Midlands	£13-16
❏	OM45604	Midland Red - Hall Green	£13-16
❏	OM45605	Midland Red - route 144	£13-16
❏	OM45606	Midland Red - route 98	£13-16
❏	OM45607	London Transport - to The Zoo (open top)	£13-16

Bristol K (lowbridge)

	Ref.	Model	Price
❏	40701	United Counties	£10-12
❏	40702	Tilling (green/cream)	£10-12
❏	40703	Premier Travel	£10-12
❏	97851	Hants & Dorset	£10-12
❏	97854	Western National	£10-12
❏	97856	West Yorkshire	£10-12
❏	97858	Caledonian	£10-12
❏	97859	Bristol Tramways	£10-12

❏ OM40701	Ensign Bus	£15

Bristol K (Utility)

❏ 43902	Southern Vectis	£12-15
❏ 43912	Chatham & District	£12-15
❏ 43921	London Transport	£10

Bristol L

❏ 40501	London Transport	£10-12
❏ 40502	Tilling (red/cream)	£10-12
❏ 97850	Merthyr Tydfil	£10-12
❏ 97852	Maidstone	£10-12
❏ 97855	United	£10-12
❏ 97860	Bath	£10-12
❏ 97867	North Western	£10-12
❏ 97868	Eastern Counties	£10-12
❏ 97869	Lincolnshire	£10-12

Bristol Lodekka F5

❏ OM40801	Southdown	£14-18
❏ OM40802	Brighton - Gilkes advert	£14-18
❏ OM40803	Brighton - Tamplins advert	£21
❏ OM40804	Alexander Fife	£14-18
❏ OM40805	United Counties	£14-18
❏ OM40806	Mac Tours	£14-18
❏ OM40807	Southdown (open top)	£14-18
❏ OM40808	Hants & Dorset	£14-18
❏ OM40809	Crosville	£14-18
❏ OM40810	Southdown BH&D (open top)	£14-18
❏ OM40811	Southern Vectis	£14-18
❏ OM40812	Bristol	£14-18
❏ OM40813	United Welsh	£14-18
❏ OM40814	Lincolnshire Road Car	£14-18
❏ OM40815	Gold Plated - 50th Anniversay Ltd Ed.	£14-18
❏ OM40816	Wilts & Dorset	£14-18
❏ OM40817	Western SMT - route 18	£14-18
❏ OM40817	Western SMT - route 19	£14-18
❏ 42301	Bristol Tower Wagon, Maidstone & District	£13

Burlingham Seagull

❏ 40301	Wallace Arnold	£16
❏ 40302	PMT	£10-12
❏ 40303	Silver Star	£10-12
❏ 40304	Boultons	£10-12
❏ 40305	Yelloways - Rochdale destination	£10-12
❏ 40305	Yelloways - Torquay destination	£27
❏ 40306	Happiways	£10-12
❏ 40307	N&C	£10-12
❏ 40308	Ribble	£10-12
❏ 40309	Seagull coaches	£10-12
❏ OM40301	Flights	£10-12
❏ OM40302	Stratford	£10-12
❏ OM40303	Dodds	£10-12
❏ OM40304	King Alfred	£10-12
❏ OM40305	Barton	£10-12
❏ OM40306	Ulsterbus - 50th Anniversary model	£33

Daimler CW Utility

❏ 43905	Green Line	£22
❏ 43908	Glasgow	£12-14
❏ 43909	Sheffield	£12-14
❏ 43914	Chester	£12-14
❏ 43916	Lytham St Annes	£12-14
❏ 43917	Yelloways	£12-14

Ref.	Model	Price Guide
❏ 43918	Southport	£12-14
❏ OM43902	London Transport - route 88	£12-14
❏ OM43904	London Transport - Epsom Races	£33
❏ OM43907	Maidstone	£12-14
❏ OM43908	Belfast	£12-14
❏ OM43911	Coventry	£17
❏ OM43912	Douglas - route 10	£12-14
❏ OM43912	Douglas - route 25	£12-14

Dennis Dart

Ref.	Model	Price Guide
❏ 42801	Kingfisher Huddersfield	£10-12
❏ 42802	Eastern National	£10-12
❏ 42804	Stevensons of Uttoxeter	£10-12
❏ 42805	Plymouth Citibus	£11
❏ 42806	London Bus lines	£10-12
❏ 42807	Bee Line	£10-12
❏ 42809	VFM	£9
❏ 42810	Orpington	£10-12
❏ 42811	Stagecoach	£10-12
❏ 42812	Brewers	£10-12
❏ 42813	Aberdeen	£14

Dennis Dart SLF (Pointer 2)

Ref.	Model	Price Guide
❏ 44702	Airport Connect	£12-14
❏ 44703	London United - route 555	£12-14
❏ 44705	Barton	£12-14
❏ 44706	Plymouth Citibus	£12-14
❏ 44707	Eireann	£12-14
❏ OM44701	Lothian	£15-18
❏ OM44702	Metroline	£15-18
❏ OM44703	Thamesdown	£15-18
❏ OM44704	Arriva Thamesworld	£15-18
❏ OM44705	Scottish Cityline	£15-18
❏ OM44706	Travel London	£15-18
❏ OM44707	Brighton & Hove - route 46	£15-18
❏ OM44707	Brighton & Hove - route 46	£15-18
❏ OM44708	UNO	£15-18
❏ OM44709	Arriva London	£15-18
❏ OM44710	Trent Barton - route V1	£15-18
❏ OM44710	Trent Barton - route V3	£15-18

East Lancashire Bodywork

Ref.	Model	Price Guide
❏ OM41101	St Helens (AEC Regent)	£15-18
❏ OM41102	Huddersfield (Daimler)	£15-18
❏ OM41103	Accrington (Leyland)	£15-18
❏ OM41104	Stockport (Leyland)	£15-18
❏ OM41105	Bolton (Daimler)	£15-18
❏ OM41106	Gtr Manchester (Leyland)	£15-18
❏ OM41107	Ramsbottom (Leyland)	£15-18
❏ OM41109	Bradford - Saltaire destination	£15-18
❏ OM41109E	Bradford - Bradford Moor destination	£15-18
❏ OM41110	Merthyr Tydfil	£15-18
❏ OM41111	Black Prince - Leeds Corn Exchange destination	£15-18
❏ OM41111	Black Prince - Morley destination	£15-18
❏ OM41112	Burnley, Colne & Nelson - Burnley destination	£19
❏ OM41112	Burnley, Colne & Nelson - Colne destination	£20

East Lancashire (modern body)

Ref.	Model	Price Guide
❏ OM42501	Ipswich	£15-18
❏ OM42502	London	£15-18
❏ OM42503	Nottingham	£15-18
❏ OM42504	Arriva Fox County	£15-18
❏ OM42505	Blackburn	£15-18
❏ OM42506	Eireann	£16

Ref.	Model	Price Guide
❏ OM42507	Brighton & Hove	£19
❏ OM42508	Isle of Man	£21
❏ OM42509	Metro Coastlines	£15-18
❏ OM42510	Delaine	£15-18
❏ OM42511	Lincolnshire Road Car	£17
❏ OM42512	Eireann - Cork	£15-18
❏ OM42513	Hackney	£15-18
❏ OM42514	Blackpool - route 14, Blackpool destination	£15-18
❏ OM42514	Blackpool - route 14, Annes Square destination	£15-18
❏ OM42515	Sanders Coaches - route 4	£15-18
❏ OM42515	Sanders Coaches - route 14	£15-18
❏ OM42516	Go Whippet	£15-18
❏ OM42517	Cumbria	£15-18
❏ OM42518	London United - route 9	£15-18
❏ OM42518	London United - route 27	£15-18

Feltham Tram

Ref.	Model	Price Guide
❏ OM40501	London Transport	£21
❏ OM40502	Leeds	£15-18
❏ OM40503	Sunderland	£15-18
❏ OM40504	Metropolitan	£15-18
❏ OM40505	London United Tramways	£15-18
❏ OM40506	Metropolitan - route 30	£15-18

Guy Arab Utility

Ref.	Model	Price Guide
❏ 43901	Oxford	£12-14
❏ 43906	Southdown	£22
❏ 43907	London Transport	£28
❏ 43910	Birmingham	£12-14
❏ 43913	Alexander & Sons	£12-14
❏ 43919	Southampton	£12-14
❏ 43920	Derby	£12-14
❏ OM43901	Llandudno & Colwyn Bay	£12-14
❏ OM43903	Bradford	£12-14
❏ OM43905	Western SMT	£12-14
❏ OM43906	Swindon	£12-14
❏ OM43909	Southdown	£12-14
❏ OM43910	East Kent	£12-14
❏ OM43913	Ribble - route 10	£12-14
❏ OM43913	Ribble - route 628	£12-14
❏ OM43914	Maidstone	£12-14

Guy Breakdown Wagon

Ref.	Model	Price Guide
❏ 41601	Bournemouth	£11
❏ 41602	Southdown	£36
❏ 42201	Guy Tower Wagon, Birmingham	£11
❏ 41801	Leyland Breakdown Wagon, Ribble	£10-12

Leyland Leopard

Ref.	Model	Price Guide
❏ 40201	Midland Red - black roof	£10-12
❏ 40203	East Kent	£10-12
❏ 40205	Ballykissangel	£10-12
❏ 97835	Ribble	£10-12
❏ 97901	Midland Red	£15
❏ 97903	Lough Swilly	£10-12
❏ 97905	Safeway Services	£10-12
❏ OM40201	Southdown	£16
❏ OM40202	Midland Red - route X92	£10-12

Leyland Lynx Mk1

Ref.	Model	Price Guide
❏ 43101	West Midlands Travel	£10-12
❏ 43102	Wycombe	£10-12
❏ 43103	City Line	£10-12
❏ 43105	Yorkshire Wollen	£10-12

☐	43106	London United	£10-12
☐	43108	Beeline	£10-12
☐	43109	Crosville Cymru	£10-12
☐	43112	Stagecoach (red/white)	£10-12
☐	43113	Brighton & Hove	£10-12
☐	43115	PMT	£10-12
☐	43117	Travel West Midlands	£10-12
☐	OM43101	London & Country	£10-12
☐	OM43102	Ribble	£10-12
☐	OM43103	Preston	£10-12

Leyland Lynx Mk2

☐	43104	Nottingham	£10-12
☐	43110	United	£10-12
☐	43111	Cardiff	£10-12
☐	43114	John Fishwick & Sons	£10-12
☐	43116	Maidstone	£10-12

Leyland PD1 (ECW)

☐	40801	Hants & Dorset	£10-12
☐	40802	Crosville	£10-12
☐	97837	North Western	£10-12
☐	97839	Eastern Counties	£10-12

Leyland PD2 (Orion body/BMMO front)

☐	40901	Chesterfield	£10-12
☐	40902	A1 Service	£10-12
☐	40903	Lytham st Annes	£10-12
☐	40904	Walsall	£10-12
☐	97944	Tynemouth/Northern Echo (Ltd Ed 15000)	£10-12
☐	OM40902	Edinburgh (aluminium finish)	£10-12

Leyland PD2 (Orion body/Leyland radiator)

☐	41101	Manchester	£10-12
☐	41102	Portsmouth	£10-12
☐	41104	Plymouth	£10-12
☐	97945	Ribble	£10-12
☐	OM40901	Nottingham	£10-12
☐	OM40903	Ulster Transport	£10-12

Leyland PD2 (Orion body/St Helens front)

☐	41103	Blackpool - Tramway Centenery	£10-12
☐	41201	Cardiff	£10-12
☐	41202	Blackpool Transport	£10-12
☐	97941	St Helens	£10-12
☐	OM40904	City of Exeter	£10-12

Leyland PD3 (single headlights)

☐	41901	Southdown - route 45	£17
☐	41909	Southdown - route 139	£16
☐	41910	A1 Services (Daimler)	£13
☐	41910	A1 Services (Scotmodel 2000)	£23
☐	OM41907	Southdown DH&D - route 2	£15

Leyland PD3 (double headlights)

☐	41902	Southdown	£10-15
☐	41903	Southdown (NBC)	£10-15
☐	41905	London Country - National Holidays advert	£10-15
☐	41906	London Country - no advert	£10-15
☐	41907	Lancaster	£10-15
☐	OM41901	Weardale	£10-15
☐	OM41904	OK Motor Services	£10-15
☐	OM41909	Southdown (NBC) - route 12	£10-15
☐	OM41910	Southdown - route 192	£10-15

| ❏ OM41911 | Boroline | £10-15 |

Leyland PD3 (open top)

❏ 42001	Southdown	£10-15
❏ 42002	Lallys of Galway	£10-15
❏ OM41902	Wallace Arnold	£10-15
❏ OM41903	London Pride	£10-15
❏ OM41905	Southdown - Beautiful Britain	£10-15
❏ OM41906	United	£10-15
❏ OM41908	Peoples Provincial	£10-15

Leyland PS1 (ECW)

❏ 40601	Western Welsh	£8-10
❏ 40602	Isle of Man	£8-10
❏ 97836	East Yorkshire	£8-10
❏ 97838	Birch Bros	£8-10
❏ OM40601	Southdown	£8-10

Leyland Olympian

❏ 43001	Wear	£17-20
❏ 43002	Crosville Happy Dragon	£17-20
❏ 43003	Go-Ahead Gateshead	£17-20
❏ 43004	Keighley	£17-20
❏ 43005	Stagecoach Scotland	£17-20
❏ 43006	North Western Bee Line	£17-20
❏ 43007	Go Coastline	£17-20
❏ 43008	Blackpool Stagecoach - United Counties	£17-20
❏ 43009	Stagecoach - United Counties	£17-20
❏ 43010	PMT	£17-20
❏ 43011	Halifax	£12-15
❏ 43013	Ribble	£12-15
❏ 43014	Southern Vectis	£19
❏ CP43001	Arriva Cymru	£12-15
❏ OM43002	Stagecoach North West	£12-15
❏ 43214	Leyland/Volvo Olympian, Capital Citybus	£17

Leyland RTW

❏ OM41701	London Transport - route 95	£18-22
❏ OM41702	Barton	£18-22
❏ OM41703	London Transport - route 41	£18-22
❏ 43903	Leyland Utility, London Transport	£13

Metrobus MCW Mk1 (single door)

❏ 45102	London Transport - route W8	£12-15
❏ OM45101	Stevensons	£12-15
❏ OM45110	West Midlands - Post Office advert	£12-15
❏ OM45115	Gtr Manchester	£12-15
❏ OM45116	Lincolnshire Road Car	£12-15
❏ OM45117	Reading Buses London Express - Heathrow destination	£12-15
❏ OM45117	Reading Buses London Express - Reading destination	£19
❏ OM45118	London Transport - route 286	£12-15

Metrobus MCW Mk1 (double doors)

❏ 45103	London Transport - route 16	£12-15
❏ 45108	London United	£12-15
❏ OM45102	London General - route 85	£12-15
❏ OM45104	London General - route 27 Cobham (Ltd Ed 500)	£27

Metrobus MCW Mk2 (single door)

❏ 45101	Yorkshire Rider	£12-15
❏ 45104	East Kent	£12-15
❏ 45105	London Transport - route 170 (double door version)	£11
❏ 45109	Stagecoach East Kent	£12-15
❏ CP45106	Go Northern	£12-15

❏ OM45103	Strathclyde	£12-15
❏ OM45105	Coventry	£12-15
❏ OM45107	Travel West Midlands	£12-15
❏ OM45109	West Bromwich	£12-15
❏ OM45110	West Midlands	£12-15
❏ OM45111	Maidstone	£12-15
❏ OM45112	Birmingham	£12-15
❏ OM45113	Wolverhampton	£12-15
❏ OM45114	Walsall	£12-15
❏ OM45119	Dublin Bus	£12-15

Neoplan Cityliner

❏ 44201	Parrys	£13-16
❏ 44202	Hallmark	£13-16
❏ 44203	Harris Holidays	£13-16
❏ 44204	Supreme Travel	£13-16
❏ 44205	Z Cars, Bristol	£13-16
❏ OM44201	Oak Hall	£13-16
❏ OM44202	Kings Ferry	£13-16
❏ OM44203	Harry Shaw	£13-16

Northern Counties Palatine II

❏ 43601	Blackpool Transport	£12-14
❏ 43602	City Line	£12-14
❏ 43603	Gtr Glasgow	£12-14
❏ 43604	Uxbridge	£17
❏ 43605	Capital Citybus	£12-14
❏ 43606	Arriva Northumbria	£12-14
❏ 43607	East Yorkshire	£12-14
❏ 43608	Badgerline	£12-14
❏ 43609	Go Coastline	£12-14
❏ 43610	Northumbria	£12-14
❏ 43611	MTL North	£12-14
❏ 43612	Nottingham	£12-14
❏ 43613	Orpington Bus - 50th Anniversay	£12-14
❏ 43614	Bristol	£12-14
❏ OM43601	Harris - Lakeside Link	£12-14
❏ OM43602	Wilts & Dorset	£12-14
❏ OM43603	Blackpool	£12-14
❏ OM43604	Kentish Bus	£12-14

Optare Delta

❏ 42901	Gateshead Supershuttle	£12-14
❏ 42902	Northumbria	£12-14
❏ 42903	Blackpool	£12-14
❏ 42904	Trent	£12-14
❏ 42905	PMT	£12-14
❏ 42906	Crosville	£12-14
❏ 42907	Edinburgh	£12-14
❏ 42908	Stagecoach - East London	£12-14
❏ 42909	Westlink	£12-14
❏ 42910	Blackpool & Fylde	£12-14
❏ 42911	Barton	£12-14
❏ 42912	South West Trains	£12-14
❏ OM42901	Metro Coastlines - Blackpool	£12-14
❏ OM42902	Wilts & Dorset	£12-14

Optare Solo

❏ 44101	Wilts & Poole - Poole destination	£12-14
❏ 44102	Go Wear	£12-14
❏ 44103	Leeds	£12-14
❏ 44104	Silver - Ltd Ed. For Optaire	£12-14
❏ 44105	Travel London	£12-14
❏ 44106	Blackpool Transport	£12-14

Ref.	Model	Price Guide
❏ 44107	Dyram Park	£12-14
❏ 44108	Wilts & Dorset - Christchurch destination	£12-14
❏ 44109	Travel West Midlands	£12-14
❏ OM44101	Blackpool Handy Bus	£12-14
❏ OM44102	Stagecoach NW	£12-14
❏ OM44103	Reading	£12-14
❏ OM44104	First Essex	£12-14
❏ OM44105	First Manchester Metro Shuttle	£12-14
❏ OM44106	Ulsterbus	£12-14
❏ OM44107	Preston	£12-14
❏ OM44108	Addenbrookes	£12-14
❏ OM44109	Strathtay Buses	£12-14
❏ OM44110	Chrome plated - 20th Anniversary	£27
❏ OM44111	Trent Barton - route 1A	£12-14
❏ OM44111	Trent Barton - route 92	£12-14
❏ OM44112	Gower Explorer - route 115	£12-14
❏ OM44112	Gower Explorer - route 117	£12-14
❏ 40102	Park Royal Trolleybus, Hastings Tramways	£12-15

Plaxton Beaver 2

Ref.	Model	Price Guide
❏ 43401	Eastern National	£10-12
❏ 43402	Stagecoach Manchester	£10-12
❏ 43403	Corgi Collector Club 1998 model	£10-12
❏ 43404	PMT	£10-12
❏ 43405	Travel Merry Hill	£10-12
❏ 43406	Trent Buses	£10-12
❏ 43407	Arriva Medway Towns	£10-12
❏ 43408	Midland Red	£10-12
❏ 43409	Trent	£10-12
❏ 43410	Midland Mainline	£10-12
❏ 43411	Sheffield Mainline	£10-12
❏ 43412	First Glasgow	£10-12
❏ 43413	First Calderline	£10-12
❏ OM43401	Stagecoach Ribble	£10-12
❏ OM43402	East Yorkshire	£10-12
❏ OM43403	Western Greyhound	£10-12

Plaxton Excalibur

Ref.	Model	Price Guide
❏ 43801	Wallace Arnold	£12-14
❏ 43802	Ulsterbus	£12-14
❏ 43803	Oxford citylink	£12-14
❏ 43804	Shearings	£12-14
❏ 43805	Flights	£12-14
❏ 43806	Virgin Rail	£12-14
❏ OM43302	Harry Shaw	£14-16
❏ OM43307	Dunn-Line	£14-16
❏ OM43309	The Airline - Oxford, Heathrow & Gatwick	£14-16
❏ OM43311	Oxford London Express	£14-16

Plaxton Panorama I

Ref.	Model	Price Guide
❏ 42401	Black & White (Daimler)	£12-14
❏ 42402	Southdown (Leyland)	£12-14
❏ 42404	Southdown - NBC white (Leyland), raised driving area	£12-14
❏ 42404	Southdown - NBC white (Leyland), flat driving area	£28
❏ 42405	Yelloway (AEC)	£12-14
❏ 42406	Timpson (Bedford)	£12-14
❏ OM42401	Highland Omnibus Ltd (Ford)	£14-16
❏ OM42402	Sheffield United (AEC)	£14-16
❏ OM42403	King Alfred (Bedford)	£14-16
❏ OM42404	Midland Red (Leyland)	£14-16
❏ OM42405	Ribble (Leyland)	£14-16
❏ OM42406	Neath & Cardiff (AEC)	£14-16
❏ OM42407	Wallace Arnold (Leyland)	£14-16
❏ OM42408	Southdown (Leyland)	£14-16

Ref.	Model	Price Guide
❑ OM42409	Lancashire United	£14-16
❑ OM42410	Yelloway (Bedford)	£14-16
❑ OM42411	Barton	£14-16
❑ OM42412	Kenzies	£14-16

Plaxton Premier

❑ 43301	Oxford Citylink	£12-14
❑ 43302	Express Shuttle	£12-14
❑ 43303	Flightlink	£12-14
❑ 43304	Eireann Eurolines	£12-14
❑ 43305	Stagecoach - Western	£12-14
❑ 43306	National Express	£12-14
❑ 43307	Epsom	£12-14
❑ 43308	Skills	£12-14
❑ 43309	Brighton & Hove	£12-14
❑ 43310	Stagecoach - Fife	£12-14
❑ 43311	Travel Bassetts	£12-14
❑ 43312	Silverdale	£12-14
❑ 43313	Plymouth	£12-14
❑ 43314	Southern - London	£12-14
❑ 43315	GNER	£12-14
❑ 43316	Scottish City Link	£12-14
❑ 43317	Jetlink	£12-14
❑ 43318	National Express - Remebrance Day	£12-14
❑ 43319	National Holidays	£12-14
❑ 43320	Robinsons	£12-14
❑ OM43301	Wallace Arnold	£14-16
❑ OM43303	Blackburn	£14-16
❑ OM43304	Elcock Reisen	£14-16
❑ OM43305	National Express - British Legion	£14-16
❑ OM43306	Scottish City Link	£14-16
❑ OM43308	Tellings	£14-16
❑ OM43310	National Express - Airport	£14-16
❑ OM43312	Wilts & Dorset - route X33	£14-16
❑ OM43313	McKindless	£14-16
❑ OM43314	Red & White	£14-16

Q1 Trolleybus (AEC, BUT & Sunbeams)

❑ 43701	London Transport - route 667	£14-17
❑ 43702	Belfast	£14-17
❑ 43703	Glasgow	£14-17
❑ 43704	Cardiff	£14-17
❑ 43705	Newcastle	£14-17
❑ 43706	Cardiff	£14-17
❑ 43707	Glasgow - route 102	£14-17
❑ 43708	London Transport - route 603	£14-17
❑ 43709	Glasgow - route 101	£21
❑ 43710	Silver plated	£14-17
❑ 43711	Huddersfield	£14-17
❑ 43712	London Transport - route 607	£14-17
❑ 43713	Nottingham	£14-17
❑ 43714	Reading	£14-17
❑ OM43701	Belfast	£14-17
❑ OM43702	Cardiff	£14-17
❑ OM43703	London Transport - route 677	£14-17
❑ OM43704	Bournemouth	£14-17
❑ OM43705	Rotherham	£14-17
❑ OM43706	Glasgow - route 101	£14-17
❑ OM43707	London Transport - route 601	£14-17

Roe Body

❑ OM41401	Teeside - North Grimsby destination	£18-20
❑ OM41401	Teeside - South Bank destination	£18-20
❑ OM41402	Northampton (Daimler)	£18-20

Ref.	Model	Price
❏ OM41403	Lincoln (Leyland) - route 2	£18-20
❏ OM41403	Lincoln (Leyland) - route 22	£18-20
❏ OM41404	Felix Motors (AEC) - Doncaster Armthorpe destination	£18-20
❏ OM41404	Felix Motors (AEC) - Moorends destination	£18-20
❏ OM41405	Maidstone (Trolleybus)	£18-20
❏ OM41406	Wolverhampton (Guy) - Wolverhapton destination	£18-20
❏ OM41406	Wolverhampton (Guy) - Bridgnorth destination	£18-20
❏ OM41407	Derby (Trolleybus) - route 11	£18-20
❏ OM41407	Derby (Trolleybus) - route 22	£18-20
❏ OM41408	Samuel Ledgard (AEC) - Ilkley destination	£18-20
❏ OM41408	Samuel Ledgard (AEC) - Leeds destination	£18-20
❏ OM41409	Sunderland (Guy) - Route 20	£18-20
❏ OM41409	Sunderland (Guy) - Route 24	£18-20

Scania Irizar PB

Ref.	Model	Price
❏ OM46201	National Express	£19
❏ OM46202	National Express - Happy St Patricks Day destination	£21
❏ OM46202	National Express - London destination	£23

Van Hool Alizee (rear window and non rear window versions)

Ref.	Model	Price
❏ 42701	Shearings - with rear window	£19
❏ 42702	National Express	£33
❏ 42703	Eireann	£28
❏ 42704	Wallace Arnold	£16
❏ 42705	OK Travel	£9
❏ 42706	Baker	£10-12
❏ 42708	Bluebird	£10-12
❏ 42709	Eavesway	£9
❏ 42710	Railair	£10-12
❏ 42711	Speedlink	£10-12
❏ 42712	Shearings - no rear window	£10-12
❏ 42713	Clarkes	£17
❏ 42714	Eurolines	£10-12
❏ 42715	Shearings - with air con	£10-12
❏ 42716	Scottish Citylink	£10-12
❏ 42717	Leger	£10-12
❏ 42718	Seagull Coaches	£10-12
❏ 42719	Stagecoach - East Kent	£10-12
❏ 42720	Evesway - Everton Football Club	£10-12
❏ 42721	Robinson & Sons	£10-12
❏ 42722	Kings Ferry	£10-12
❏ 42723	Seagull	£10-12
❏ 42724	Ellen Smith	£10-12
❏ 42725	Western National	£10-12
❏ 42726	Shearings Holidays	£10-12
❏ 42727	Lewis Coaches	£10-12
❏ 42728	Parks	£10-12
❏ 42729	British Airways	£10-12
❏ OM42701	Whippet Coaches	£10-12
❏ OM42702	Shearings - 2001 livery	£17

Van Hool T9

Ref.	Model	Price
❏ OM45901	Kenzies	£17
❏ OM45901	Shearings	£18-22
❏ OM45902	National Express - Leicester destination	£18-22
❏ OM45902	National Express - London destination	£18-22
❏ OM45903	Fraser Eagle	£18-22
❏ OM45904	Caelloi Motors - 50th Anniversary	£31
❏ OM45905	West Coast Motors - Cambeltown destination	£18-22
❏ OM45905	West Coast Motors - Glasgow destination	£18-22
❏ OM45906	Goodwins	£18-22
❏ OM45907	WA Shearings	£18-22
❏ OM45908	Maynes	£18-22
❏ OM45909	Shearings Grand Tourer	£18-22

❏ OM45910	Bartons	£18-22
❏ OM45911	Bibby's	£18-22

Weymann BUT Trolleybus

❏ 40101	Maidstone/Odds Timber (Ltd Ed 8100)	£15
❏ 40103	Walsall	£10-12
❏ 40104	Bradford Corporation	£10-12
❏ 40105	Bradford - Coronation	£10-12
❏ 40106	Maidstone & District	£10-12
❏ 40107	Brighton - route 43	£10-12
❏ 40111	Notts & Derby	£10-12
❏ 40113	Brighton - route 42	£10-12
❏ OM40101	Maidstone Corporation - Park Wood destination	£10-12

Wright Eclipse Gemini

❏ OM41201	Demonstrator	£16-20
❏ OM41202	Arriva london	£16-20
❏ OM41203	Travel West Midlands	£16-20
❏ OM41204	Harrogate	£16-20
❏ OM41205	London General	£16-20
❏ OM41206	First North East	£16-20
❏ OM41207	Yellow Buses	£16-20
❏ OM41208	London United	£16-20
❏ OM41209	Yorkshire Coastliner	£16-20
❏ OM41210	Travel Dundee	£16-20
❏ OM41211	First London	£16-20
❏ OM41212	Arriva - Back the Bid	£16-20
❏ OM41213	Travel London	£22
❏ OM41214	First Leicester	£16-20
❏ OM41215	East Yorkshire - Cottingham, The Lawns destination	£16-20
❏ OM41215	East Yorkshire - Cottingham, Beverley Rd destination	£16-20
❏ OM41216	Go North East - route X10	£16-20
❏ OM41217	Witch Way - Manchester destination	£16-20
❏ OM41217	Witch Way - Nelson destination	£16-20
❏ OM41218	Arriva Midlands - route 31	£16-20
❏ OM41218	Arriva Midlands - route 31a	£16-20

Wright Solar Fusion Bendy Bus

❏ OM41301	Go Ahead North East	£30-35
❏ OM41302	Nottingham	£30-35
❏ OM41303	First Southampton	£30-35
❏ OM41304	First London	£24
❏ OM41305	Dublin	£30-35
❏ OM41306	First York - route 3	£30-35
❏ OM41306	First York - route 8	£30-35
❏ OM41307	Doigs - 50th Anniversary	£37
❏ OM41308	First Bath	£30-35

Wrightbus Urban Eclipse

❏ OM46001	Bare metal	£27
❏ OM46002	Whitelaws - Hamilton destination	£17-22
❏ OM46002	Whitelaws - Stonehouse destination	£17-22
❏ OM46003	Lothian	£17-22
❏ OM46004	Arriva Fastrack - Temple Hill destination	£17-22
❏ OM46005	Arriva - Shires & Essex, Dunstable destination	£17-22
❏ OM46005	Arriva - Shires & Essex, Luton destination	£17-22
❏ OM46006	First Glasgow - Baillieston destination	£17-22
❏ OM46006	First Glasgow - Faifley destination	£17-22
❏ OM46007	Rosendale - Accrington destination	£17-22
❏ OM46007	Rosendale - Rochdale destination	£17-22
❏ OM46008	Reading - Overdown Rd destination	£17-22
❏ OM46008	Reading - Westward Glen destination	£17-22
❏ OM46009	Arriva - Gravesend destination	£15
❏ OM46010	Ulster Metro - route 3a	£17-22

☐ OM46010	Ulster Metro - route 11	£17-22

Bus Sets

☐ 45001	Dorset Delights	£17-22
☐ 45002	Varsity	£17-22
☐ 45003	Stagecoach	£17-22
☐ 97851	Crosville	£12-15
☐ 97055	Thames Valley	£12-15
☐ 97057	Southdown	£12-15
☐ 97095	Lancashire Holiday	£12-15
☐ 97096	Capital & Highlands	£12-15
☐ 97097	Bridges & Spires	£12-15
☐ OM99146	Midland Red 2pce set	£27
☐ OM99156	Blackpool Balloon Tram - 70th Anniversary 2pce set	£39
☐ OM99166	Solent Blue Line 2pce set	£29
☐ OM99172	Metrobus 2pce set	£33
☐ OM99186	Route Through Time 3pce set	£50
☐ OM99191	Tamar Link 2pce set	£37
☐ OM49901	Plaxton Centenary 4pce set	£88

ORIENTAL (Hong Kong) OMNIBUS COLLECTION

☐ 32701	AEC Regent (1:64), Kowloon Motor Bus - open top	£17
☐ OM41108	AEC Regent MkV (1:76), KMB	£14

AEC Routemaster 1:64

☐ 32401	Hong Kong Peak Tramway	£14
☐ 32702	Kowloon Motor Bus - Christmas	£17

AEC Regent II (Weymann) 1:76

☐ 40407	Kowloon Motor Bus - route 3	£27
☐ 40408	Kowloon Motor Bus - route 1	£33

Dennis Dart 1:76

☐ 42803	Citybus	£10-13
☐ 42808	Kowloon Motor Bus	£10-13
☐ 42814	New Lantao Bus - standard packaging	£11
☐ 42814	New Lantao Bus - special bus pack containing badges	£69
☐ 44701	Dennis Dart SLF (1:76), Citybus	£19

Dennis Trident 1:76

☐ 44301	Kowloon Motor Bus	£37
☐ 44302	Citybus	£19
☐ 44303	KMB - route 30	£45
☐ 44401	New World - First Bus	£59
☐ 44402	New World - Wish Bus	£33
☐ 44403	Nathan Road	£14
☐ 44405	KMB Longwin Bus	£25-30
☐ 44406	KMB Green	£25-30
☐ 44407	KRCR	£72
☐ OM45801	Alexander ALX (1:76), Citybus Cityflyer	£19

Duple Metsec Trident 1:76

☐ 44501	Cityflyer - fleet no. 2112, route A21	£29
☐ 44502	Cityflyer - Smart Connection decal	£41
☐ 44502	Cityflyer -no decal	£14-18
☐ 44503	Cityflyer - route 21	£27
☐ 44504	Citybus	£14-18
☐ 44505	New World - 100th new bus	£15
☐ 44506	KMB - Millenium Bus	£21
☐ 44507	Citybus - www	£14-18
☐ 44508	Citybus Millenium - chrome	£26
☐ 44509	Citybus - Hong Kong Transport	£19
☐ 44510	Citybus - Year of the Dragon	£19
☐ 44511	KMB - Gold	£31

❏ 44512	KMB - Millenium	£14-18
❏ 44513	Citybus - Greener Bus	£14-18
❏ OM44501	Citybus - Year of the Horse	£14-18

Guy Victory 1:76
❏ 44801	China Motor Bus	£14-18
❏ 44802	KMB	£21
❏ 44803	China Motor Bus - Driver Recruitment	£14-18
❏ 44804	KMB - Shung Shui	£25-30
❏ 44805	Farwell Victory	£25-30
❏ 44806	CMB - LV1	£25-30
❏ OM44801	KMB - Series 3	£25-30

Leyland Atlantean 1:76
❏ 44601	Citybus - Happy Valley	£24
❏ 44602	Singapore Bus	£14-18
❏ 44603	Citybus - Network 26	£14-18
❏ OM25602	KMB	£28
❏ 43012	Leyland Olympian (2-axle) 1:76, Ocean Parl	£16

Leyland Volvo Olympian (3-axle) 1:76
❏ 43201	Kowloon Motor Bus	£49
❏ 43202	Kowloon & Canton Railway	£14-18
❏ 43202	Kowloon & Canton Railway - 10th Anniversary	£45
❏ 43203	Handover - KMC	£31
❏ 43204	Handover - Citybus	£14-18
❏ 43205	Citybus	£14-18
❏ 43206	China Motor Bus	£14-18
❏ 43207	Handover - KMB	£14-18
❏ 43208	Long Win	£14-18
❏ 43209	Buspac	£88
❏ 43210	Handover (China Motor Bus)	£14-18
❏ 43211	New World First Bus - 'This bus has ears'	£21
❏ 43212	New World First Bus - 'Did you recognise me'	£21
❏ 43213	New World First Bus - 'We must stop meeting....'	£24
❏ 43214	Capital Citybus	£14-18
❏ 43215	KMB - Year of the Tiger	£66
❏ 43216	CMB - Airport Express	£26
❏ 43217	Stagecoach - Hong Kong	£14-18
❏ 43218	KRCR - red/white/grey	£26
❏ 43219	Singapore Super Bus - 25th Anniversary	£14-18
❏ 43220	KMB - white	£23
❏ 43221	KMB - Year of the Rabbit	£22
❏ 43222	KMB - Dragon Boat	£14-18
❏ 43223	Friends of KMB	£14-18
❏ 43224	KMB - 50th Anniversary	£14-18
❏ 43225	KMB - Year of the Dragon	£29
❏ 43226	KMB - Year of the Snake	£31
❏ OM43201	KMB - Year of the Horse	£26
❏ OM43202	KMB - Year of the Goat	£14-18

Leyland PD3 1:76
❏ 41904	China Motor Bus - red/cream	£37
❏ 41980	China Motor Bus - blue/cream	£16
❏ OM44801	Leyland Victory Mk2 (1:76), KMB - Series 3	£22

MAN Volgren (3-axle) 1:76
❏ OM45401	HK Citybus	£41
❏ OM45402	HK Citybus	£22
❏ OM45403	Citybus - Year of the Snake	£24
❏ OM45404	Citybus - Standard	£18
❏ OM45405	Citybus - Special	£18
❏ OM45201	Berkhof (1:76), KMB	£21

Metrobus (1:76)

❏ 45107	China Motor Bus - blue/cream	£21
❏ OM45108	KMB	£16-20

Metrobus 1:76

❏ 91705	Kowloon Motor Bus	£13-16
❏ 91710	Kowloon - Canton Railway	£13-16
❏ 91907	China Motor Bus	£13-16

Van Hool Alizee 1:76

❏ 42707	Citybus - Chinese & HK number plates	£12
❏ 42707	Citybus - HK number plates only	£39

Bus Sets

❏ 45004	China Motor Bus 2pce set	£49
❏ 45005	East & West 2pce set	£39
❏ 45006	Citybus Network 2pce set	£36
❏ 45007	Ocean Park Citybus 2pce set	£34

TRAMS
Double Deck (closed top/open front)

❏ C992/1	Leeds	£8-12
❏ C992/2	Glasgow	£8-12
❏ C992/3	London County Council	£8-12
❏ C992/4	Blackpool	£8-12
❏ C992/5	Bradford	£8-12
❏ C992/6	Southampton	£8-12
❏ C992/7	Birmingham	£8-12
❏ C992/8	London Transport (made in GB)	£8-12
❏ 36801	Glasgow	£8-12
❏ 36802	Leeds	£8-12
❏ 97260	Birkenhead	£8-12
❏ 97261	South Shields	£8-12
❏ 97267	Grimsby	£8-12
❏ 97268	London - LCC to New Cross destination	£8-12
❏ 97270	Bolton	£8-12
❏ 98153	London Transport (made in China)	£8-12
❏ CC25205	Nottingham	£8-12

Double Deck (closed top/closed front)

❏ D37/1	Penny Post Anniversary	£12-15
❏ D993/1	Portsmouth	£12-15
❏ D993/2	Dover	£12-15
❏ 98154	Dover (made in China)	£12-15
❏ D993/3	Coventry	£12-15
❏ 36701	London Transport - Highbury	£12-15
❏ 36702	Dundee	£12-15
❏ 36704	London Transport - Last Tram Week	£12-15
❏ 36705	Edinburgh	£12-15
❏ 36706	Sheffield - Crookes destination	£12-15
❏ 36707	Leeds	£12-15
❏ 36708	London Transport - Ilford Broadway	£12-15
❏ 36709	Queen Mother Centenary - blue/gold	£12-15
❏ 36710	Sunderland - Vernons	£12-15
❏ 36711	Birmingham - Inglis Biscuits	£12-15
❏ 36712	Queen Mother Centenary - maroon/gold	£12-15
❏ 97262	Blackpool - Winter Gardens	£12-15
❏ 97264	Cardiff	£12-15
❏ 97265	Belfast	£12-15
❏ 97273	Blackpool Pleasure Beach	£12-15
❏ 97285	Leicester	£12-15
❏ 97286	Sunderland	£12-15
❏ 97287	Nottingham	£12-15
❏ 97288	Sheffield - Vulcan Rd destination	£12-15

	Ref.	Model	Price Guide
❑	97293	Newcastle	£12-15
❑	97294	Birmingham	£12-15
❑	97296	Liverpool	£12-15
❑	-	London Transport - Bassett Lowke advert	£12-15
❑	CC25202	London Transport - Wisk advert	£12-15
❑	CC25203	Liverpool	£12-15
❑	CC25204	Bolton	£12-15
❑	CC25207	Gold plated	£21

Double Deck (open top/open front)

	Ref.	Model	Price Guide
❑	C991/1	London	£12-15
❑	C991/2	Blackpool	£12-15
❑	C991/3	Bath	£12-15
❑	C991/4	Bournemouth	£12-15
❑	C991/5	Burton & Ashby	£12-15
❑	C991/6	Croydon	£12-15
❑	C991/7	National Garden Festival	£12-15
❑	36601	Wallasey	£12-15
❑	36602	Leicester	£12-15
❑	36603	West Hartlepool	£12-15
❑	36604	Croydon - Rawling & Oldfied adverts	£12-15
❑	D991/8	Llandudno	£12-15
❑	97266	Paisley	£12-15
❑	97269	Plymouth	£12-15
❑	97290	Hull	£12-15
❑	97291	South Shields	£12-15
❑	97295	Sheffield	£12-15
❑	97365	Blackpool Tower	£12-15
❑	98150	Lowestoft	£12-15
❑	98151	Southern Metropolitan	£12-15
❑	CC25201	Belfast	£12-15
❑	CC25206	Queen Elizabeth II Golden Jubilee	£12-15
❑	CC25208	XV11 Commonwealth Games	£12-15

Single Deck

	Ref.	Model	Price Guide
❑	C990/1	Southampton	£12-15
❑	C990/2	Sheffield	£12-15
❑	C990/3	Derby	£12-15
❑	C990/4	Wolverhampton	£12-15
❑	C990/6	Maidstone	£12-15
❑	36901	Blackpool	£12-15
❑	36902	Darlington	£12-15
❑	36903	Blackpool	£12-15
❑	97263	Ashton under Lyne	£12-15

BUSES 1:50 SCALE

	Ref.	Model	Price Guide
❑	97018	AEC Regal IV (Weymann), Dundee	£13

AEC Routemaster

	Ref.	Model	Price Guide
❑	35001	London Transport	£17-20
❑	35002	London Transport - RM664, silver	£17-20
❑	35003	Shillibeer	£17-20
❑	35004	London Transport - Golden Jubilee	£17-20
❑	35005	London Transport - Jacobs	£17-20
❑	35006	Liverpool - Beatles Collection	£17-20
❑	35007	London Transport - Typhoo	£17-20
❑	35007H	London Transport - Hamleys	£17-20
❑	35008	Stagecoach	£17-20
❑	35009	Blackpool	£17-20
❑	35010	London Transport - Queen Mothers Centenary	£17-20
❑	CC25901	Metroline	£17-20
❑	CC25902	Queen Elizabeth II	£17-20
❑	CC25903	Gold plated	£27
❑	CC25904	London Transport - Routemaster 50th Anniversary	£31

| --- | --- | --- |
☐ CC25905	Delaine	£29
☐ CC25906	London Transport - Londons New Tube	£29
☐ CC25907	London Transport - route 159	£32
☐ CC25908	London Transport - route 6	£17-20

AEC Routemaster (open top)
☐ 35101	Original London Sightseeing Tour	£17
☐ 35102	London Coaches	£21

AEC RT/Leyland RTL
☐ CC26101	London Transport - route 62	£35
☐ CC26102	London Transport - route 27	£35
☐ CC26103	London Transport - route 457, green	£55

Bristol K Utility
☐ 97853	Bristol	£15-19
☐ 97857	London Transport	£15-19
☐ 97875	Cardiff - 75th Anniversary	£22

Daimler CW Utility
☐ 35201	Green Line	£18-22
☐ 97820	West Bromich	£18-22
☐ 97822	Derby	£18-22
☐ 97827	Sheffield	£18-22
☐ 97829	Douglas	£18-22
☐ 97336	Glasgow	£18-22
☐ CC25502	Aberdeen	£18-22

Daimler Fleetline
☐ 97824	Birmingham	£18-22
☐ 97826	Manchester	£18-22
☐ 97828	Rochdale - Guernsey Tomatoes advert	£18-22
☐ 97828	Rochdale - Corgi Heritage Centre advert	£40

Guy Arab
☐ 34301	Swindon	£14-18
☐ 97198	Southdown - route 37A	£27
☐ 97199	Birkenhead	£14-18
☐ 97201	Birmingham	£14-18
☐ 97202	Maidstone	£14-18
☐ 97203	London Transport	£14-18
☐ 97204	Coventry	£14-18
☐ 97205	Bournemouth	£14-18
☐ 97206	Northern	£14-18
☐ 97208	Yorkshire	£14-18
☐ 97209	Walsall	£14-18
☐ 97310	Southampton	£14-18
☐ 97311	Midland Red	£14-18
☐ 97312	Wolverhampton	£14-18
☐ 97313	Paisley	£14-18
☐ 97314	Oxford	£14-18
☐ 97315	London Transport - grey	£14-18
☐ CC25501	Southdown - route 12	£27

Leyland Atlantean
☐ 97230	Ribble	£18-22
☐ 97231	Hull	£18-22
☐ 97232	Wallasey	£18-22
☐ 97341	Maidstone	£18-22
☐ CC25601	Scout Motor Services	£30-35

Leyland Atlantean (open top)
☐ 97233	Devon General	£20-25
☐ 33501	Guide Friday - Brighton Tour	£20-25

Leyland Olympian

❏ 34801	Western Welsh	£14
❏ 34802	Sheffield	£20-25
❏ CC25801	Birmingham	£33

Leyland Tiger Cub (Weymann)

❏ 34901	Manchester	£19
❏ 97810	Leicester	£14
❏ 97363	Edinburgh	£14
❏ 97364	North Western	£14
❏ CC25802	King Alfred	£34

Thorneycroft

❏ C858	Sandemans - 4 top deck support	£14-18
❏ C858	Sandemans - 8 top deck supports	£14-18
❏ C858/1	Beaulieu Motor Museum - red canopy	£14-18
❏ C858/1	Beaulieu Motor Museum - red canopy	£14-18
❏ C858/2	Douglas	£14-18
❏ C858/3	Cambrian	£14-18
❏ C858/4	Vanguard	£14-18
❏ C858/6	London & NW Railway	£14-18
❏ C858/7	Oakeys	£14-18
❏ C858/10	Schwepppes Tonic	£14-18
❏ C858/11	Great Eastern Railway	£14-18
❏ C884	Beer is Best	£14-18
❏ C885	Thomas Tilling - 4 top deck supports	£14-18
❏ C885	Thomas Tilling - 8 top deck supports	£14-18
❏ C888	Portsmouth	£14-18
❏ C975	City	£14-18
❏ 96985	East Surrey	£14-18
❏ 96986	Brighton & Hove	£14-18
❏ 96987	Schweppes Ginger Beer	£14-18
❏ 96988	Beamish	£14-18
❏ 96989	Cricklewood destination	£14-18
❏ 96991	Sheffield	£14-18
❏ 96992	Norfolk	£14-18
❏ 96993	Yelloways	£14-18
❏ 96994	South Wales	£14-18
❏ 96996	Thomas Tilling	£14-18

COACHES 1:50 SCALE
AEC Regal

❏ 33201	Finglands	£12-15
❏ 97020	Wye Valley Motors	£12-15
❏ 97021	MacBraynes	£12-15
❏ 97180	Grey/green	£12-15
❏ 97181	Timpsons	£12-15
❏ 97184	Sheffield	£12-15
❏ 97185	West Riding	£12-15
❏ 97186	Grey Cars	£12-15
❏ 97187	Hanson	£12-15
❏ 97189	Oxford	£12-15
❏ 97190	Ledgard	£12-15
❏ 97191	Rosslyn Motor Co	£12-15
❏ 97193	Carneys	£12-15
❏ 97194	Hardings	£12-15
❏ 97196	Stanley Field	£12-15
❏ 97197	Western Welsh	£12-15
❏ 98161	Eastern Counties	£12-15
❏ 98162	Wallace Arnold	£12-15
❏ 33302	Albion Valliant Duple Coach, Western SMT	£26

Bedford OB

❏ C949/1	Norfolk - small destination blinds	£55

| --- | --- | --- |
❏ C949/1	Norfolk - large destination blinds	£49
❏ C949/2	Royal Blue - small destination blinds	£234
❏ C949/2	Royal Blue - small destination blinds	£55
❏ C949/3	Blue Bird	£36
❏ C949/4	Grey Cars	£20-25
❏ C949/5	Crosville	£20-25
❏ C949/6	Southdown	£20-25
❏ C949/7	Eastern	£20-25
❏ C949/8	South Midlands	£20-25
❏ C949/9	Premier - dk blue bonnet	£20-25
❏ C949/9	Premier - non dk blue bonnet version	£20-25
❏ C949/11	East Yorkshire	£20-25
❏ C949/12	Classic	£17
❏ C949/13	Hants & Sussex	£20-25
❏ C949/14	Wallace Arnold	£20-25
❏ C949/15	MacBraynes	£36
❏ C949/17	Greenslades	£10-12
❏ C949/18	Devon General	£10-12
❏ C949/19	Southern Vectis	£20-25
❏ C949/22	Boultons	£11
❏ C949/23	Howards	£14
❏ C949/24	Southern National	£14
❏ C949/25	Eastern National - green line on base	£14
❏ C949/25	Eastern National - non green line version	£20-25
❏ C949/26	West Yorkshire	£13-16
❏ C949/27	British Railways - Medsted destination	£13-16
❏ C949/30	Western National	£13-16
❏ C949/31	British Railways - Bristol destination	£13-16
❏ 33801	Pearce & Crump	£13-16
❏ 33802	Malta - yellow, white roof	£13-16
❏ 33803	British Railways	£13-16
❏ 33804	Guinness	£13-16
❏ 97100	Isle of Man Tours	£13-16
❏ 97101	Scilly Isles	£13-16
❏ 97102	Skills of Nottingham - green bonnet	£13-16
❏ 97102	Skills of Nottingham - non green bonnet version	£13-16
❏ 97104	Bronte Tours	£13-16
❏ 97105	Felix Coaches	£13-16
❏ 97106	Bibby's	£13-16
❏ 97107	Murgatroyd	£13-16
❏ 97108	Granville Tours	£13-16
❏ 97109	Whittaker Tours	£13-16
❏ 97111	Meredith	£13-16
❏ 97113	Warburtons	£13-16
❏ 97115	Seagull	£13-16
❏ 97347	Malta - green	£27
❏ 98163	Grey Green (Ltd Ed 14000)	£10
❏ 98164	Edinburgh	£13-16

Bedford Val Coach (CONNOISSEUR Collection)

❏ 35301	Yelloway	£19
❏ 35303	SELNEC (Ltd Ed 3600)	£21
❏ 35304	Smiths Tours	£21
❏ 35305	Wallace Arnold	£24
❏ 33301	Bristol Duple Coach, Southern National	£22

Burlingham Seagull

❏ 34101	Ribblesdale	£13-16
❏ 97170	Woods	£13-16
❏ 97171	Neath & Cardiff	£13-16
❏ 97172	Stratford Blue (Ltd Ed 5000)	£32
❏ 97173	Ribble	£28
❏ 97174	Yelloway	£31

❏ 97175	Don Everall	£13-16
❏ 97176	King Alfred	£13-16
❏ 97177	North Roadway	£13-16
❏ 97178	Coliseum	£13-16
❏ 97179	Banfields	£13-16
❏ 97342	West Coast Motor Services	£13-16
❏ 97340	Trent	£13-16

Daimler Duple Coach

❏ 97821	Swan	£13-16
❏ 97823	Blue Bus Service	£13-16
❏ 97825	Burwell & District	£13-16
❏ 97830	Scout	£13-16
❏ 33101	Dennis Lancet Coach, Smiths of Reading	£22

Leyland Tiger

❏ 97192	Ribble	£22
❏ 97210	Maypole	£13-16
❏ 97211	Bartons	£13-16
❏ 97212	Ellen Smith	£13-16
❏ 97213	Red & White	£13-16
❏ 97214	Skills	£13-16
❏ 97216	Delaine	£13-16

TROLLEYBUS 1:50 SCALE
Karrier W

❏ 97316	Ipswich	£18-20
❏ 97870	Newcastle	£18-20
❏ 97871	Bradford	£18-20
❏ 34701	Nottingham	£18-20
❏ 34703	Derby	£18-20

Sunbeam

❏ 34702	Ashton under Lyme	£18-20
❏ 97800	Reading	£18-20
❏ 97801	Maidstone	£18-20

Other 1:50th Scale Bus related models

❏ 97404	Land Rover - Maidstone	£8
❏ 16102	Scammell Highwayman Crane - Southdown	£19
❏ 22502	Bedford TK Platform Trailer - MacBraynes	£17
❏ 55605	Diamond T Wrecker - Blackpool	£16
❏ 96837	Morris 1000 Van - Maidstone	£8
❏ 96895	Morris J Van - Birmingham 'General Manager' lettering	£8
❏ 98895	Morris J Van - Birmingham 'Genetal Manager' misspelling	£17
❏ 96756	Morris Minor - Bristol	£8
❏ 98165	Ford Cortina - London Transport	£8
❏ 96888	Morris J Van - Southdown	£8

GIFT SETS

❏ D4/1	Transport of the early 1950s 2pce set	£37
❏ D41/1	Bartons 1950s Transport 2pce set	£17
❏ C89	Baxters 60 Years of Transport 3pce set	£89
❏ 36501	Bartons 1950s Transport 2pce set	£19
❏ 96990	AEC 2pce set	£22
❏ 97050	Regent Bus 2pce set	£15
❏ 97052	Devon General 2pce set	£39
❏ 97053	York Brothers 2pce set	£22
❏ 97057	Southdown 2pce set (Ltd Ed 10000)	£19
❏ 97061	Coventry 2pce set	£22
❏ 97063	Yelloways 2pce set	£31
❏ 97069	Whittle Buses 2pce set	£22
❏ 97070	Silver Service 2pce set	£27
❏ 97071	Devon 2pce set	£21

❏ 97072	Gosport & Fareham 2pce set	£21
❏ 97075	South Wales 2pce set	£23
❏ 97076	W Alexander & Sons Ltd 2pce set	£41
❏ 97077	East Lancashire 2pce set	£41
❏ 97078	From Corkhills to Vanenburg 2pce set	£21
❏ 97079	Premier Buses 2pce set	£21
❏ 97741	Jersey Island Transport 2pce set	£14
❏ 97750	East Kent 2pce set	£21

ROUTEMASTER Fully closed version, LT red (1:64 SCALE)

❏ C463	British Meat	£3-6
❏ C467	Selfridges – route 12	£3-6
❏ C467	Army & Navy	£3-6
❏ C469	Swan & Edgar	£9
❏ C469	Beatties, Taylor & McKenna - route 8	£3-6
❏ C469	BTA - route 11, Welcome to Britain	£3-6
❏ C469	BTA - route 24, Welcome to Britain	£3-6
❏ C469	Cobham Museum	£9
❏ C469	Evening Standard - route 15	£3-6
❏ C469	Evening Standard - route 16	£3-6
❏ C469	Gamleys - route 11	£3-6
❏ C469	Hamleys - route 6, 3 clowns advert	£3-6
❏ C469	Hamleys - route 6, 4 clowns advert	£3-6
❏ C469	Hamleys - route 6, 5 clowns advert	£3-6
❏ C469	Hamleys - route 16 (logo change)	£3-6
❏ C469	Harlands	£11
❏ C469	Jacobs	£3-6
❏ C469	London Marriott Hotel	£8
❏ C469	Selfridges - route 15	£3-6
❏ C469	Visit London Zoo	£3-6
❏ C469	Whatman Paper	£9
❏ C469	Underwoods	£3-6
❏ C473	Gamleys - route 16	£3-6
❏ C488	Beatties - route 25	£3-6
❏ C559	Roland Keyboards/Auto Spares	£3-6
❏ C596	Harrods	£3-6
❏ 32301	London Transport Museum - route 7	£3-6
❏ 32301	Evening Standard - route 15 (small advert)	£3-6
❏ 32301	Collectors Choice - route 7 Meadowhall	£3-6
❏ 91760	Evening Standard - route 15 (large advert)	£3-6
❏ 91760	London Aquarium - route 15	£3-6
❏ 91760	White Rose Shopping Centre - route 15, Mosley Leeds	£3-6
❏ TY82301	Route 13	£3-6
❏ CC82304	Queen Elizabeth II 75th Birthday	£3-6
❏ TY82308	Hamleys	£3-6
❏ TY82311	Routemaster 50th Anniversary	£3-6
❏ -	Routemaster London Transport - route 159 (various liveries)	£3-6

Closed top, LT non red colour versions

❏ C469	Shillibeer - Addis advert	£3-6
❏ C469	London Transport 1933 - 1983 - silver roof	£9
❏ C471	Silver Jubilee - See More London advert	£3-6
❏ C471	Silver Jubilee - Woolworths advert	£3-6
❏ C471	Silver Jubilee - Mintex advert	£28
❏ C471	Culture Bus	£3-6
❏ C479	London Crusader	£3-6
❏ C482	Shillibeer - Leeds Permanent advert	£3-6
❏ C483	London Shoplinker	£3-6

Other liveries

❏ C460	Bolton Evening News	£3-6
❏ C464	Motor Show	£3-6
❏ C469	Aero - cream	£3-6
❏ C469	Barrett - 2-tone blue	£3-6

	Ref.	Model	Price Guide
❑	C469	Blackpool Illuminations	£11
❑	C469	Buy Before You Fly - green/yellow	£3-6
❑	C469	Corning Glass Centre	£3-6
❑	C469	Cowes Stamp & Model Shop	£3-6
❑	C469	Dion - Saves You Money	£3-6
❑	C469	Dion - Saves You More	£3-6
❑	C469	Cadbury's Double Decker - orange	£3-6
❑	C469	Eagle Star - black	£3-6
❑	C469	Eagle Star - blue/white	£3-6
❑	C469	Essex Organ Studios	£3-6
❑	C469	Farnham Maltings	£3-6
❑	C469	Gloucester Toy & Train Sale	£3-6
❑	-	Great Book of Corgi	£11
❑	C469	Great Western Railway	£3-6
❑	C469	Reading Express	£3-6
❑	C469	Jolly Giant - green/yellow	£3-6
❑	C469	Just a Second	£3-6
❑	C469	Lion Bar - green	£3-6
❑	C469	Liverpool Garden Festival	£3-6
❑	C469	Llandrindod Wells Victorian Festival	£3-6
❑	C469	Manchester Lions Club	£3-6
❑	C469	Midland Bus Museum	£3-6
❑	C469	New Corgi Company - red	£3-6
❑	C469	Norbrook Motors - blue	£3-6
❑	C469	Old Smugglers	£3-6
❑	C469	OXO - orange/white	£3-6
❑	C469	Redgates - cream/brown	£9
❑	C469	Stretton Spring Water	£3-6
❑	C469	TDK - blue/white	£3-6
❑	C469	Trowbridge Toys & Models	£3-6
❑	C469	Twinings	£3-6
❑	C469	John Webb Toy Fairs	£3-6
❑	C469	World Airways - cream/brown	£3-6
❑	C470	Pentel	£3-6
❑	C475	Take Off from Bristol	£3-6
❑	C476	British Telecom	£3-6
❑	C476	White Label	£3-6
❑	C477	Busby Bus	£3-6
❑	C480	East Yorkshire	£3-6
❑	C481	BEA	£3-6
❑	C485	Isle of Wight County Press - Southern Vectis advert	£3-6
❑	C485	Isle of Wight County Press - 2 people on advert	£3-6
❑	C485	ML Electrics	£3-6
❑	C488	New Corgi Company - green	£3-6
❑	C492	MA Rapport	£3-6
❑	C521	Haig	£3-6
❑	C523	Swapmeet Toys & Models	£3-6
❑	C524	Stevensons	£3-6
❑	C527	Timbercraft	£3-6
❑	C529	1985 Calendar	£3-6
❑	C530	Yorkshire Post	£3-6
❑	C567	See More London - white	£3-6
❑	C571	The Times - maroon	£3-6
❑	C572	The Times - blue	£3-6
❑	C574	Blackpool Centenary	£3-6
❑	C580	Andrex	£3-6
❑	C583	Manchester Evening News	£3-6
❑	C590	Medic Alert	£3-6
❑	C627	Model Motoring	£3-6
❑	C633	Hospital Radio	£3-6
❑	C628	Polio	£3-6
❑	C638	Weetabix - blue lettering on white background	£3-6
❑	C638	Weetabix - white lettering on blue background	£3-6

❏	32303	Cadbury's Double Decker - orange/purple	£3-6
❏	32304	The Beatles - Penny Lane destination, green	£3-6
❏	TY82302	Ireland - route 65	£3-6
❏	CC82305	Harrods	£3-6
❏	CC82306	2002 Manchester Commonwealth Games	£3-6
❏	CC82308	Hamleys	£3-6

Routemaster (open top)

❏	C469	Blackpool Pleasure Beach	£3-6
❏	C469	Hamleys	£3-6
❏	C469	London Sightseeing Tour	£3-6
❏	C469	Old Holbourn	£3-6
❏	C469	Manchester United	£3-6
❏	C469	TDK - orange	£3-6
❏	C469	TDK - yellow	£3-6
❏	C469	Disneyland	£3-6
❏	C478	Sundecker	£3-6
❏	C486	Culture Bus	£3-6
❏	C558	Radio victory	£3-6
❏	C570	Bus Collectors Society	£3-6
❏	C591	Medic Alert	£3-6
❏	C625	Cityrama	£3-6
❏	C625	Sightseeing	£3-6
❏	-	Guernseybus	£3-6
❏	32402	City Tour - Guide Friday	£3-6
❏	32403	Original London Sightseeing Tour	£3-6
❏	32403	Chelsea 1997 FA Cup Winners	£12
❏	32404	London Pride	£3-6
❏	60036	Hamleys (part of LT1 set)	£3-6
❏	91765	Happy Dragon	£3-6
❏	-	Houses of Parliament/Tower Bridge	£3-6
❏	91766	Original London Sightseeing Tour	£3-6
❏	CC82307	XVII Commonwealth Games	£3-6
❏	TY82303	Dublin - Guide Friday	£3-6

Metrobus

❏	C675/1	West Midlands Travel Timesaver - silver	£5-10
❏	C675/2	Reading Transport Goldline	£5-10
❏	C675/2	Yorkshire Traction Fastlink	£5-10
❏	C675/3	West Midlands Travel - blue/cream	£5-10
❏	C675/4	Beatties - route 25	£5-10
❏	C675/5	Beeline	£5-10
❏	C675/7	West Midlands Travel - black, Hitachi advert	£5-10
❏	C675/9	Newcastle Busways - no advert	£5-10
❏	C675/10	Beatties - route 109	£5-10
❏	C675/12	Maidstone - mid green version	£5-10
❏	C675/12	Maidstone - dark green version	£5-10
❏	C675/13	East Kent - various routes	£5-10
❏	C675/14	GM Buses	£5-10
❏	C675/15	Go Ahead - National Garden Festival	£5-10
❏	C675/16	Strathclyde	£5-10
❏	C675/17	PMT	£5-10
❏	32501	Travel West Midlands - route 101	£8-12
❏	91700	Gold Rider	£8-12
❏	91701	Midland Fox	£8-12
❏	91702	London Airbus	£8-12
❏	91703	Bradford	£8-12
❏	91705	Atlantic Park	£8-12
❏	91706	Kowloon Motor Bus	£8-12
❏	91710	Kowloon - Canton Railway	£8-12
❏	91839	Badgerline	£8-12
❏	91842	Strathay	£8-12
❏	91843	Cardiff	£8-12

	Ref.	Model	Price Guide
❑	91844	Nottingham	£8-12
❑	91846	Crosline Coastliner	£8-12
❑	91847	East Kent	£8-12
❑	91848	Yorkshire Rider - Evening Post	£8-12
❑	91849	Yorkshire Rider - Cars are Bad News	£8-12
❑	91850	West Midlands Travel Employee Owned - green	£8-12
❑	91851	Reading Buses - 90th Anniversary	£8-12
❑	91852	Stevensons	£8-12
❑	91853	Leeds - Bradford	£8-12
❑	91854	Halifax - Open Day	£8-12
❑	91855	West Yorkshire	£8-12
❑	91856	Sunderland Busways	£8-12
❑	91857	Newcastle Busways - Fenwick advert	£8-12
❑	91858	Leeds - Bradford	£8-12
❑	91859	Halifax - Open Day	£8-12
❑	91861	Todmorden	£8-12
❑	91862	Bradford - Whizzwheels	£8-12
❑	91863	Huddersfield	£8-12
❑	91864	Grey Green	£8-12
❑	91868	Huddersfield Tramways	£8-12
❑	91706	Superliner	£8-12
❑	91709	West Midlands Travel - blue/silver (Ltd Ed 5500)	£8-12
❑	97802	Hull	£8-12
❑	97803	Cleveland	£8-12
❑	-	China Motor Bus	£8-12

AEC Regent

	Ref.	Model	Price Guide
❑	C599	Nottingham	£7-11
❑	D599	Beatties - open top, white	£7-11
❑	C599/1	London Transport - Wisk soap	£7-11
❑	D599/1	Western	£7-11
❑	C599/2	Eastbourne	£12
❑	C599/3	Leicester	£14
❑	C599/4	Glasgow	£7-11
❑	C599/5	Rhonnda	£7-11
❑	C599/6	Morcombe	£7-11
❑	C599/7	Bradford	£7-11
❑	D599/10	Brighton	£7-11
❑	D599/11	Dublin	£7-11
❑	D599/12	RAF	£7-11
❑	D599/13	Halifax	£7-11
❑	C634	London Transport - Maples	£7-11
❑	C643	Newcastle	£7-11
❑	96980	Stevensons	£3-5
❑	96982	Rochdale	£7-11
❑	96983	Liverpool	£7-11
❑	97001	PMT	£7-11
❑	97002	Sheffield	£7-11
❑	97003	West Bridgeford	£7-11
❑	97062	Oxford	£7-11
❑	91704	Atlantic Park - open top	£7-11
❑	-	1993 Corgi Collector Club model	£7-11

Various Scales
Plaxton Paramount

	Ref.	Model	Price Guide
❑	C769	Club Cantabrica	£46
❑	C769	Rapide National Express	£15
❑	C769/4	SAS Flybussen	£13
❑	C769/5	Global	£8-12
❑	C769/6	Pohjolan Lijikenne	£43
❑	C769/7	Bluebird Express	£8-12
❑	C769/8	Scottish Citylink	£8-12
❑	C770	Holiday Tours	£17

Ref.	Model	Price Guide
❑ C771	Air France	£16
❑ C772	SAS Flybussen	£8-12
❑ C773	Green Line	£8-12
❑ C774	Reading	£14
❑ C775	Oxford City Link	£8-12
❑ C776	Skills	£8-12
❑ C777	Taylors	£15
❑ C791	PTT	£19
❑ C792	Gatwick Flightline	£8-12
❑ C793/1	Intasun Express	£8-12
❑ 32601	Bluebird - route 47	£8-12
❑ 32602	National Express - route 353	£8-12
❑ 32605	British Airways Holidays	£8-12
❑ 91707	SAS Airlanda	£8-12
❑ 91905	Nottingham	£8-12
❑ 91909	Finnair	£8-12
❑ 91911	Applebys	£8-12
❑ 91912	East Kent	£8-12
❑ 91913	Voyager	£8-12
❑ 91914	Heathrow/Gatwick Speedlink	£8-12
❑ 91915	Tellus - Midland Red	£8-12
❑ 91916	East Yorkshire Diplomat	£8-12
❑ 91917	Highwayman	£8-12
❑ 91918	Southend Transport	£8-12
❑ 91919	Shearings	£8-12
❑ 91922	Greenline - route 711	£8-12
❑ 91922	Greenline - route 758	£8-12
❑ TY84101	Eireann	£8-12
❑ TY84103	National Express - route 353	£8-12

Routemasters in Exile - Gift Sets

Ref.	Model	Price Guide
❑ 97066	Scotland 4pce set	£27
❑ 97067	The Midlands 4pce set	£25
❑ 97068	The North 4pce set	£23
❑ 97074	The South 4pce set	£29
❑ 33001	Routemasters Around Britains 4pce set	£31
❑ 97064	Blackpool 3pce set	£22
❑ 97051	Invicta 2pce set	£12
❑ 97065	Stagecoach 3pce set	£19

METTOY

Tin plate & Clockwork Bus 1:36 Scale

Ref.	Model	Price Guide
❑ MT00101	Routemaster - London Transport - route 8B, red (Ltd Ed 2006)	£45
❑ MT00103	London Transport - route 15	£50
❑ MT00106	London Country - route 465, green (Ltd Ed 1000)	£55
❑ MT00107	London Transport - open top Sightseeing Tour	NPA

Tin plate & Clockwork Taxi 1:24 Scale

Ref.	Model	Price Guide
❑ MT00102	Black	£34
❑ MT00104	Burgandy/black	£45
❑ MT00105	Silver	NPA

EMERGENCY VEHICLES

EMERGENCY - FIRE
1:50 SCALE
AEC Pumper

❑ 21801	Blackpool	£14-18
❑ 21802	Hong Kong	£14-18
❑ 97355	Nottinghamshire	£14-18
❑ 97356	Nottinghamshire County Council - Dunkirk	£14-18
❑ 97357	Herfordshire	£14-18
❑ 97358	Cleveland	£14-18
❑ 97359	Dublin	£14-18
❑ 97360	Rotherham, yellow	£14-18

AEC with ladder

❑ 22001	West Yorkshire	£14-18
❑ 97352	Stoke	£14-18
❑ 97353	Dublin	£14-18
❑ 97361	New Zealand	£14-18
❑ 97385	Cardiff	£14-18
❑ 97386	Bristol	£14-18
❑ CC10305	Hereford & Worcester	£27
❑ CC10306	Nottinghamshire	£27
❑ CC10307	Perth (Western Australia)	£25-30
❑ CC10310	Wiltshire	£25-30
❑ CC10304	AEC HCB Angus Water Loader, Leciester	£24
❑ CC60304	Bedford QLD, Army Fire Service	£15

Bedford S

❑ 19201	Cambridgeshire	£15
❑ CC10901	Clywd County (dropside)	£15

Dennis (1:50 scale)

❑ CC13001	Blackburn (Ltd Ed 6500)	£20-25
❑ CC13002	Bradford (Ltd Ed 5000)	£20-25
❑ CC13004	Leics & Rutland	£20-25
❑ CC13005	Coventry (Ltd Ed 3200)	£20-25
❑ CC13006	Hartlepool	£20-25
❑ CC13007	Birmingham	£20-25
❑ CC13008	Belfast	£20-25
❑ CC13011	Stoke-on-Trent	£20-25
❑ CC55106	Diamond T Wrecker, Glamorgan	£32
❑ CC02301	Ford Transit Mk1, Warwickshire	£11

Simon Snorkel

❑ 32001	Cheshire	£25
❑ 97392	West Glamorgan	£25
❑ 97399	Cleveland	£25
❑ CC13003	Merseyside	£25
❑ CAN13009	Bedfordshire 50th Anniversary	£35-40
❑ AN13010	Gold plated 50th Anniversary model	£82

Other Fire Related Vehicles

❑ 5604	AFS Bedford CA van	£8-12
❑ 7106	West Sussex Land Rover	£8-12
❑ 7301	AFS Land Rover	£8-12
❑ 7410	Hampshire Land Rover	£8-12
❑ 7411	Cliff Rescue Landrover	£8-12
❑ 7417	Leics & Rutland Land Rover	£8-12
❑ 19701	AFS Bedford S	£8-12
❑ 22703	Foam Salvage Unit Bedford	£8-12
❑ 98475	Fire Marshall VW	£8-12
❑ 96906	Blackburn Bedford CA	£8-12

EMERGENCY - AMBULANCE

❑ CC06301	Birmingham	£15-20
❑ CC06302	Croydon	£15-20
❑ CC06303	Nottingham	£15-20
❑ CC06304	Northern Ireland	£15-20
❑ CC06305	LCC	£15-20

EMERGENCY - POLICE

❑ 30307	Thames Trader Control Unit	£8-12
❑ 96685	Jaguar Mk2, white/orange bonnet, Staffs	£8-12
❑ 96744	Morris Minor, reg BDA 327H	£8-12
❑ 96744	Morris Minor, reg BDA 327H, white, Leics	£8-12
❑ 96744	Morris Minor, reg AMP 33H	£8-12
❑ 96759	Morris Minor, reg EMB 327F, Merthyr Tidfil	£8-12
❑ 96855	Morris Minor van, green/yellow, Wilts	£8-12
❑ 96873	Morris Minor Traveller, Edinburgh	£8-12
❑ 96883	Morris J van, Met Police	£8-12
❑ 96920	Bedford Dormobile (renumbered 98106)	£8-12
❑ 96951	Mini van, lt blue	£8-12
❑ 96956	Mini van, dk blue, Surrey	£8-12
❑ 98141	Mini Cooper, Liverpool	£8-12
❑ C703/1	Morris Minor, reg PES 645J (with wipers)	£8-12
❑ C703/1	Morris Minor, reg PES 645J (without wipers)	£8-12
❑ C706/1	Jaguar Mk2, black	£8-12
❑ D708/6	Ford Cortina (renumbered 96500)	£8-12
❑ CC85516	New Mini Cooper, NSW	£8-12
❑ CC85517	New Mini Cooper, Royal Canadian	£8-12
❑ CC85518	New Mini Cooper, Munich	£8-12
❑ CC85519	New Mini Cooper, Durham	£8-12

Emergency Sets

❑ D13/1	Police Minor vans 2pce set	£18-22
❑ D75/1	Police Cars 3pce set (Ford Zephyr, Jaguar & Morris Minor)	£27
❑ 8004	Hampshire Police 2pce set (Bedford & Morris)	£22
❑ 8005	Stockport Borough 2pce Mini van & Morris Minor set (Ltd Ed 4800)	£19
❑ 8006	Thames Valley 2pce set (Mini van & Bedford)	£20
❑ 97331	La France 2pce set (Scottdale & South River)	£18-22
❑ 97697	Leics & Rutland 2pce set (Jaguar Mk2 & Morris Minor van)	£18-22
❑ 97698	Metropolitan police 2pce set (Bedford coach & Morris Minor)	£18-22
❑ 97721	Durham Police 2pce set (Jaguar Mk2 & Mini)	£18-22
❑ 97772	South Glamorgan Police 2pce set (Morris Minor van & MGA)	£18-22
❑ CC99152	Proud to Serve (Hants) 4pce set plus 4 badges (Ltd Ed 1800)	£52

Other Emergency Vehicles

❑ 7102	Mersey Tunnel Breakdown Land Rover	£8-12
❑ 96854	Morris Motors Ltd pick-up	£8-12
❑ 97337	Fawley Refinery Mini van	£8-12
❑ CC07407	RAF Airfield Crash Rescue Land Rover	£8-12
❑ CC13519	Central Scotland Fire & Rescue Volvo	£40

AVIATION ARCHIVE (1:144 Scale)

	Ref.	Model	Price
❏	47101	Douglas C47 Skytrain - USAF	£10-15
❏	47102	Douglas DC3 - American Airlines	£10-15
❏	47103	Douglas C47A - Aer Lingus	£10-15
❏	47104	Douglas DC3 Dakota - BEA	£10-15
❏	47105	Douglas DC3 - Eastern Airlines	£10-15
❏	47106	Douglas DC47A - Battle of Britain Memorial Flight	£10-15
❏	47107	Douglas DC3 - Air Atlantic	£10-15
❏	47108	Douglas DC3 - KLM	£10-15
❏	47109	Douglas DC3 - Lufthansa	£10-15
❏	47110	Douglas DC3 - Air France	£10-15
❏	47111	Douglas DC3 Dakota - Berlin Airlift	£10-15
❏	47112	Douglas EC47P Skytrain - USAF	£10-15
❏	47114	Douglas C47B Dakota - RAF Transport Command	£10-15
❏	47201	Avro York - Resin pre production model	£29
❏	47201	Avro York - Skyways	£15-20
❏	47202	Avro York - BOAC	£15-20
❏	47203	Avro York - Dan Air	£15-20
❏	47204	Avro York - RAF Kings Flight	£15-20
❏	47205	Avro York - Berlin Airlift	£15-20
❏	47206	Avro York - French Air Force	£15-20
❏	47301	Avro Lancaster - Battle of Britain Memorial Flight	£15-20
❏	47302	Avro Lancaster - Coastal Command	£15-20
❏	47303	Avro Lancaster - RCAF	£15-20
❏	47304	Avro Lancaster - 617 Squadron	£15-20
❏	47306	Avro Lancaster - Mickey the Moocher	£15-20
❏	47307	Avro Lancaster - Indian 9th Squadron Salabini	£15-20
❏	47401	Avro Lancaster - Trans Canada Air Lines	£15-20
❏	47402	Avro Lancaster - BOAC	£15-20
❏	47403	Avro Lancaster - Berlin Airlift	£15-20
❏	47501	Lockheed Constellation - TWA	£15-20
❏	47502	Lockheed Constellation - Quantas	£15-20
❏	47503	Lockheed Constellation - Air India	£15-20
❏	47504	Lockheed Constellation - KLM	£15-20
❏	47505	Lockheed Constellation - Braniff International	£15-20
❏	47506	Lockheed Constellation - USAF	£15-20
❏	47507	Lockheed Constellation - Eastern Airlines	£15-20
❏	47508	Lockheed Constellation - Pan Am	£15-20
❏	47509	Lockheed Constellation - Military Air Transport Service	£15-20
❏	47601	Vickers Viscount 700 - BEA	£15-20
❏	47602	Vickers Viscount 800 - Parcelforce	£15-20
❏	47603	Vickers Viscount 800 - Continental	£15-20
❏	47604	Vickers Viscount 800 - Lufthansa	£15-20
❏	47605	Vickers Viscount 700 - British Eagle	£15-20
❏	47606	Vickers Viscount 806 - Virgin	£15-20
❏	47607	Vickers Viscount 800 - BEA	£15-20
❏	47608	Vickers Viscount 806 - BA	£15-20
❏	47609	Vickers Viscount 836 - BMA	£15-20
❏	48101	Boeing Stratocruiser - Pan Am	£20-25
❏	48102	Boeing KC97L - Illinois Air Guard	£20-25
❏	48103	Boeing C97G - Delaware Air Guard	£20-25
❏	48104	Boeing C97A - Military Air Transport Service	£20-25
❏	48105	Boeing Stratocruiser - BOAC	£20-25
❏	48106	Boeing Stratocruiser - Transocean	£20-25
❏	48201	Boeing B17G Flying Fortress - Bit O Lace	£20-25
❏	48203	Boeing Fortress Mk2A - Coastal Command	£20-25

Ref.	Model	Price Guide
☐ 48204	Boeing B17 Flying Fortress - Memphis Belle	£20-25
☐ 48205	Boeing B17G - Sentimental Journey	£20-25
☐ 48301	Avro Vulcan B2 - 44 Squadron	£15-20
☐ 48302	Avro Vulcan B2 - 617 Dam Busters Squadron	£15-20
☐ 48303	Avro Vulcan B2 - XH558	£15-20
☐ 48304	Avro Vulcan B2 - XM655	£15-20
☐ 48305	Avro Vulcan B2 - XL426 Southend Preservation	£15-20
☐ 48401	Lockheed Hercules - RAF	£15-20
☐ 48402	Lockheed Hercules - US Navy Blue Angels	£15-20
☐ 48403	Lockheed Hercules - RAF	£15-20
☐ 48404	Lockheed Hercules - US Coast Guard	£15-20
☐ 48405	Lockheed Hercules - RAF Desert Storm	£15-20
☐ 48406	Lockheed Hercules - USAF Vietnam camouflage	£15-20
☐ 48501	De Havilland Comet - BEA	£15-20
☐ 48502	De Havilland Comet - Dan Air	£15-20
☐ 48503	De Havilland Comet - RAF Transport Command	£15-20
☐ 48504	De Havilland Comet - BOAC	£15-20
☐ 48505	De Havilland Comet - Boscombe Down	£15-20
☐ 48506	De Havilland Comet - BEA Airtours	£15-20
☐ 48601	Bristol Britannia - Laker Airways	£15-20
☐ 48602	Bristol Britannia - BOAC	£15-20
☐ 48603	Bristol Britannia - Monarch	£15-20
☐ 48604	Bristol Britannia - RAF Transport Command	£15-20
☐ 48605	Bristol Britannia - Caledonian	£15-20
☐ 48701	Victor - Bruntingthorpe	£29
☐ 48702	Victor - RAF (white)	£15-20
☐ 48703	Victor - RAF (camouflaged)	£15-20
☐ 48801	Short Sunderland - RAF Coastal Command	£15-20
☐ 48802	Short Sunderland - BOAC	£15-20
☐ 48803	Short Sunderland - Royal Australian Air Force	£15-20
☐ 48804	Short Sunderland - RAAF 461 Squadron	£15-20
☐ 48805	Short Sunderland - 230 Squadron	£15-20
☐ 48901	Boeing B29 - Enola Gay	£15-20
☐ 48902	Boeing B29 - RAF Washington	£15-20
☐ 48903	Boeing B29 Super Fortress with Bell Helicopter	£23
☐ 49501	Battle of Britain Memorial 3pce set	£48
☐ 49502	USSF 3pce set	£39
☐ 49503	BMMF 2pce set	£19
☐ 49504	USAAF Little Friends 2pce Fighter Escort set	£16
☐ 49506	Confederate Airforce 3pce set	£36
☐ 49507	Battle of Britain Special 2pce set	£23
☐ AA30001	Douglas DC3 - Continental Airlines	£15-20
☐ AA30002	Douglas R4D5 US Navy Que Sera Sera	£16
☐ AA30003	Douglas C47 - RAF	£15-20
☐ AA30004	Douglas DC3 - Pan Am	£15-20
☐ AA30005	Douglas C47 - Royal Aircraft Establishment, Farnbourough	£15-20
☐ AA30006	Douglas C47 - USAF	£15-20
☐ AA30007	Douglas DC3 - South African Airways	£15-20
☐ AA30008	Douglas DC3 - Eddie Stobart	£15-20
☐ AA30010	Douglas C47 - 101st Airborne	£15-20
☐ AA30011	Douglas C47 - Battle of Britain Memorial Flight	£15-20
☐ AA30012	Douglas DC3 - Western Airlines	£15-20
☐ AA30013	Douglas Dakota - 24 Squadron	£15-20
☐ AA30014	Douglas DC3 - Air Atlantique	£15-20
☐ AA30015	Douglas C47D - Tunisia (1943)	£15-20
☐ AA30101	Avro Lancaster - SEAF	£15-20
☐ AA30102	Avro Lancaster NX611B Mk7	£15-20
☐ AA30103	Avro Lancaster - Admiral Prune	£15-20

Ref.	Model	Price Guide
❏ AA30104	Avro Lancaster - Flight Lt Bill Reid	£15-20
❏ AA30401	Lockheed L749 Constellation - BOAC	£15-20
❏ AA30402	Lockheed VC121A Constellation - Columbine	£27
❏ AA30403	Lockheed L749 Constellation - Air France	£32
❏ AA30404	Lockheed L749 Constellation - Trans World Airlines	£44
❏ AA30501	Vickers Viscount 800 - Aer Lingus	£23-28
❏ AA30502	Vickers Viscount 700 - United Airlines	£23-28
❏ AA30503	Vickers Viscount 800 - British Air Ferries	£23-28
❏ AA30504	Vickers Viscount 806 - North East Airlines	£23-28
❏ AA30505	Vickers Viscount 745 - Capital Airlines	£23-28
❏ AA30506	Vickers Viscount 803 - KLM	£23-28
❏ AA30507	Vickers Viscount 838 - Royal Aircraft Establishment	£23-28
❏ AA30508	Vickers Viscount 756 - George Bass	£23-28
❏ AA30509	Vickers Viscount - Empire Test Pilot School	£23-28
❏ AA30510	Vickers Viscount 802 - BEA Scottish Airways	£36
❏ A31001	Boeing Stratocruiser - North West Airlines	£20-25
❏ A31002	Boeing C97G - Angel of Deliverance	£20-25
❏ A31101	Boeing B17G - 214 Squadron	£20-25
❏ A31102	Boeing B17 Flying Fortress - Memphis Belle	£20-25
❏ A31103	Boeing B17 Flying Fortress - Yankee Doodle	£20-25
❏ A31104	Boeing B17 Flying Fortress - Memphis Belle	£20-25
❏ A31105	Boeing B17F- Knock Out Dropper	£20-25
❏ AA31201	Avro Vulcan - 617 Dambusters Squadron	£28
❏ AA31202	Avro Vulcan - Falklands War issue	£33
❏ AA31203	Avro Vulcan - 50 Squadron	£36
❏ AA31204	Avro Vulcan - 27 Squadron	£29
❏ AA31301	Lockheed Hercules - Operation Deep Freeze	£20-25
❏ AA31303	Lockheed Hercules - RAAF 37 Squadron	£20-25
❏ AA31304	Lockheed Hercules - Gunship	£20-25
❏ AA31305	Avro Vulcan - Falklands War issue	£20-25
❏ AA31306	Lockheed Hercules - Spectre Gunship	£20-25
❏ AA31307	Lockheed Hercules - RCAF	£16
❏ AA31308	Lockheed Hercules - US Navy 3 Squadron	£20-25
❏ AA31310	Lockheed Hercules - Delta Airlines	£20-25
❏ AA31311	Lockheed Martin - RAF Lyneham	£20-25
❏ AA31401	Comet 4 - Royal Aircraft Establishment (Ltd Ed 2200)	£23
❏ AA31402	DH Comet - United Arab Airlines	£20-25
❏ AA31403	DH Comet - BOAC	£20-25
❏ AA31501	Bristol Britannia 102 - Britannia	£20-25
❏ AA31502	Bristol Britannia 312F - Team Spirit	£37
❏ AA31503	Bristol Britannia 102 - BKS	£20-25
❏ AA31504	Bristol Britannia 324 - Cunard	£20-25
❏ AA31505	Bristol Britannia 307 - British United Airways	£20-25
❏ AA31506	Bristol Britannia 102 - BOAC	£20-25
❏ AA31507	Bristol Britannia SRS314 - Canadian Pacific Airlines	£20-25
❏ AA31508	Bristol Britannia - El Al	£58
❏ AA31601	Handley Page Victor - Falklands	£20-25
❏ AA31602	Handley Page Victor - Lusty Lindy	£20-25
❏ AA31603	Handley Page Victor - 55 Squadron	£20-25
❏ AA31604	Handley Page Victor - 543 Squadron	£20-25
❏ AA31701	Short Sunderland - 330 Squadron	£20-25
❏ AA31702	Short Sunderland - BOAC	£20-25
❏ AA31703	Short Sunderland - Black Peter	£20-25
❏ AA31704	Short Sunderland - 204 Squadron	£20-25
❏ AA31705	Short Sunderland - 201 Squadron	£20-25
❏ AA31801	Boeing B29 - 58th Bomb Wing Esso Express	£20-25
❏ AA31802	Boeing B29 - Hawg Wild	£20-25
❏ AA31803	Boeing B29 - Enola Gay	£30-35

Ref.	Model	Price Guide
☐ AA31804	Tupolev B29 - Russian Air Force	£30-35
☐ AA31805	Boeing B29 - Atomic Tom	£30-35
☐ AA32901	Boeing 137C - Air Force One	£21
☐ AA32902	Boeing 707 - Trans World Airlines	£15
☐ AA32903	Boeing 707 - BA	£20-25
☐ AA32904	Boeing 707 - Braniff International Airways	£12
☐ AA32905	Boeing 707 - BOAC	£15-20
☐ AA32906	Boeing 707 - Pan Am	£15-20
☐ AA32907	Boeing 707 - American Airlines	£15-20
☐ AA32908	Boeing 707 - XVII Commonwealth Games	£15-20
☐ AA32909	Boeing 707 - Quantas	£15-20
☐ AA32910	Boeing 707 - Cathay Pacific	£15-20
☐ AA32911	Boeing 707 - USAF MATS	£15-20
☐ AA32912	Boeing 707 - Dan Air	£15-20
☐ AA32913	Boeing 707 - USAF AWACS	£15-20
☐ AA32915	Boeing 707 - 8th & 23rd Squadrons	£15-20
☐ AA32916	Boeing 707 - British Caledonian	£15-20
☐ AA33501	Boeing B52 Stratofortress - 54.2672	£47
☐ AA33502	Boeing B52 Stratofortress - Diamond Lill	£45
☐ AA33503	Boeing B52 Stratofortress - Duxford	£54
☐ AA33504	Boeing B52 Stratofortress - USAF Research Aircraft	£61
☐ AA33505	Boeing B52 Stratofortress - 328th Squadron	£40-50
☐ AA33506	Boeing B52 Stratofortress	£40-50
☐ AA33507	Boeing B52 Stratofortress - 449th Bomb Wing	£60
☐ AA34604	Handley Page Victor - 543 Squadron	£40-50
☐ AA35101	Lockheed Super Constellation - National Airlines	£20-25
☐ AA35102	Lockheed Super Constellation - US Navy Blue Angels	£20-25
☐ AA35103	Lockheed Super Constellation - USAF Vietnam	£20-25
☐ AA35105	Lockheed Super Constellation - KLM	£20-25
☐ AA35602	Nimrod - Kinloss Wing	£20-25
☐ AA37001	Vickers VC10 - Falklands	£40-50
☐ AA37002	Vickers VC10 - BA	£40-50
☐ AA37003	Vickers VC10 - Brize Norton	£40-50
☐ AA38001	Fairchild Thunderbolt - USAFE	£40-50
☐ AA99134	V Bomber 2pce set	£40-50
☐ AA99148	Douglas C47, P47D & Mustang P51D 3pce set	£27
☐ AA99176	Lockheed Hercules & Pavehook Helecopter 2pce set	£42
☐ AA99190	Boeing Strathofreighter - 121st Refuelling Wing	£30-35

1:72 SCALE

Ref.	Model	Price Guide
☐ 49001	Spitfire Mk1 - Adolph Milan	£20
☐ 49002	Supermarine Spitfire Mk2A - OC Tangmere Wing	£27
☐ 49003	Spitfire Mk2 - Garfield Weston (Ltd Ed 4800)	£23
☐ 49004	Spitfire Mk1 - Brian Carbury	£22
☐ 49005	Spitfire Mk1 - 54 Squadron (Ltd Ed 5600)	£24
☐ 49101	Hawker Hurricane Mk1 - 85 Squadron	£17
☐ 49102	Hawker Hurricane Mk1 - Stanford Tuck	£24
☐ 49103	Hawker Hurricane Mk1 - 261 Squadron	£23
☐ 49104	Hawker Hurricane Mk1 - 87 Squadron (Ltd Ed 5600)	£19
☐ 49201	Messerschmitt 109E - Hauptmann Hans Von Hahn	£25-30
☐ 49202	Messerschmitt 109E - Schlageter Gallana	£65
☐ 49203	Messerschmitt 109E - 7JG51	£44
☐ 49204	Messerschmitt 109E - Desert	£43
☐ 49205	Messerschmitt 109E - Von Werpa	£47
☐ 49301	Mustang P51D - John Landers (Ltd Ed 6500)	£20-25
☐ 49302	Mustang P51D - 363rd Fighter Group	£20-25
☐ 49303	Mustang P51D - Confederate Air Force	£20-25
☐ 49401	Lightning - 56 Squadron	£20-25

Ref.	Model	Price Guide
❏ 49402	Lightning - RAF Aerobatics Team	£20-25
❏ 49403	Lightning - 5 Squadron	£20-25
❏ 49505	Battle of Britain Dog Fight 2pce set	£20-25
❏ 49801	Hawker Hunter - 79 Squadron	£20-25
❏ 49802	Hawker Hunter - Black Arrows	£20-25
❏ 49803	Hawker Hunter	£10-15
❏ AA30003	Corsair - 1835 Squadron	£25-30
❏ AA30006	Douglas C47 Dakota - USAF	£25-30
❏ AA30701	Hawker Hurricane - BD930	£10-15
❏ AA31901	Supermarine Spitfire - 276 Air Sea Rescue Squadron	£30
❏ AA31902	Supermarine Spitfire - 249 Sqaudron, Takali	£30
❏ AA31903	Supermarine Spitfire - 303 Sqaudron	£97
❏ AA31904	Supermarine Spitfire - Neville Duke (Ltd Ed 5500)	£25-30
❏ AA31905	Supermarine Spitfire - Brian Lane	£25-30
❏ AA31906	Supermarine Spitfire - US Scout Cruiser	£25-30
❏ AA31907	Supermarine Spitfire - Robert Stanford Tuck	£25-30
❏ AA31908	Supermarine Spitfire - Peter Durnford	£25-30
❏ AA31909	Supermarine Spitfire - 452 Sqaudron	£10-15
❏ AA31910	Spitfire - Clive Caldwell	£25-30
❏ AA31911	Spitfire - 302 Sqaudron	£25-30
❏ AA31912	Spitfire - Royal Aeronautical Garden Party	£25-30
❏ AA31913	Spitfire - 52nd Fighter Group	£10-15
❏ AA31914	Spitfire - G Beurling	£25-30
❏ AA31915	Spitfire - John Kent	£25-30
❏ AA31916	Supermarine Spitfire - Johnnie Johnson	£10-15
❏ AA31917	Supermarine Spitfire - Robert Gibbes	£25-30
❏ AA31919	Supermarine Spitfire 50th Anniversary model - Adolph Sailor Milan	£47
❏ AA31920	Supermarine Spitfire 50th Anniversary gold plated issue	£128
❏ AA31921	Spitfire Merlin engine	£25-30
❏ AA31924	Supermarine Spitfire - 92 Sqaudron	£25-30
❏ AA31925	Supermarine Spitfire - 411 Sqaudron	£25-30
❏ AA31927	Supermarine Spitfire - Russian Air Force	£25-30
❏ AA31928	Supermarine Spitfire - 212 Sqaudron	£25-30
❏ AA32001	Hawker Hurricane Mk2 - 174 Squadron	£39
❏ AA32002	Hawker Hurricane Mk1 - 213 Squadron night fighter	£49
❏ AA32003	Hawker Hurricane Mk2 - 6th Squadron	£10-15
❏ AA32004	Hawker Hurricane Mk2 - 242 Squadron	£25-30
❏ AA32005	Hawker Hurricane Mk2 - Last of the Many	£39
❏ AA32006	Hawker Hurricane Mk2 - 258 Squadron	£25-30
❏ AA32007	Hawker Hurricane Mk2 - Operational Training Unit	£25-30
❏ AA32008	Hawker Hurricane Mk2 - William McKnight	£25-30
❏ AA32009	Hawker Hurricane Mk2 - 6th Squadron	£10-15
❏ AN32011	Hawker Hurricane Mk2 50th Anniversary Model - Peter Townsend	£44
❏ AA32101	Messerschmitt 109E	£47
❏ AA32102	Messerschmitt 109E - Helmut wick	£69
❏ AA32103	Messerschmitt 109E - Grunherz	£10-15
❏ AA32104	Messerschmitt 109E - Eduard Neumann	£10-15
❏ AA32105	Messerschmitt 109E - Ludwig Franzisket	£10-15
❏ AN32107	Messerschmitt 109E 50th Anniversary model - Hans Von Hahn	£40-50
❏ AA32108	Messerschmitt 109E - Tropical	£40-50
❏ AA32111	Messerschmitt 109E - Duxford Preservation Society	£40-50
❏ AA32201	Mustang P51D - Old Crow (Ltd Ed 5600)	£29
❏ AA32202	Mustang P51D - Hun Hunter	£15-20
❏ AA32203	Mustang P51D - Bunnie	£15-20
❏ AA32204	Mustang P51D - Petie 2nd	£15-20
❏ AA32205	Mustang P51D - Cripes All Mighty	£15-20
❏ AA32206	Mustang P51D - 19 Squadron	£15-20
❏ AA32207	Mustang P51D - Nooky Booky 3	£15-20
❏ AA32208	Mustang P51D - Gentleman Jim	£15-20

Ref.	Model	Price Guide
❏ AA32209	Mustang P51D - 12th Fighter Bomber Squadron	£15-20
❏ AA32211	Mustang P51D - AP Tacon	£15-20
❏ AA32212	Mustang P51D - Tempus Fugit	£15-20
❏ AA32217	Mustang P51K - 112 Squadron	£15-20
❏ AN32224	Mustang P51D 50th Anniversary - Big Beautiful Doll	£43
❏ AA32301	English Electric Lightning - Tigers Aeronautical Team	£35-40
❏ AA32302	English Electric Lightning - 19 Squadron	£35-40
❏ AA32303	English Electric Lightning - 226 Operational Unit	£35-40
❏ AA32304	English Electric Lightning - 11th Squadron	£46
❏ AA32305	English Electric Lightning - 111th Squadron	£35-40
❏ AA32306	English Electric Lightning - 23rd Squadron	£29
❏ AA32307	BAC Electric Lightning	£35-40
❏ AA32308	English Electric Lightning - 56 Squadron	£35-40
❏ AA32401	Harrier - Falklands	£27
❏ AA32402	Harrier - Royal Navy	£28
❏ AA32403	Harrier - US Marines	£15
❏ AA32404	Harrier - 1969 Transatlantic Race	£18
❏ AA32405	Harrier 50th Anniversary model - 899 Squadron	£27
❏ AA32406	Harrier - 809 Squadron	£34
❏ AA32407	Harrier - Winter exercise camouflage	£34
❏ AA32408	Harrier - NASA	£10-15
❏ AA32409	Harrier - No. 233 OCU	£10-15
❏ AA32410	Harrier - 800 Naval Air Squadron	£10-15
❏ AA32411	Harrier - No.1 Squadron	£15-20
❏ AA32501	Junkers JU87B-2 Stuka	£30
❏ AA32502	Junkers JU87R2 Stuka (Ltd Ed 5500)	£27
❏ AA32503	Junkers JU87 - Eastern Front	£15-20
❏ AA32504	Junkers JU87 - Tropical	£15-20
❏ AA32505	Junkers JU87 - S2 & AP	£15-20
❏ AA32506	Junkers JU87 - North Africa (1941)	£15-20
❏ AA32507	Junkers JU87 - Bulgaria (1941)	£15-20
❏ AA32513	Junkers JU87 - RAF	£15-20
❏ AA32601	Avro Lancaster - 467 Squadron	£50-60
❏ AA32602	Avro Lancaster - Mickey the Moocher	£95
❏ AA32603	Avro Lancaster - 44 Squadron	£70
❏ AA32604	Avro Lancaster - Admiral Prune (Ltd Ed 2800)	£178
❏ AA32605	Avro Lancaster - Royal Canadian Air Force	£50-60
❏ AA32606	Avro Lancaster - Royal Canadian Air Force	£50-60
❏ AA32607	Avro Lancaster - G for George	£50-60
❏ AA32608	Avro Lancaster - Dambusters raid	£95
❏ AA32609	Avro Lancaster - 617 Squadron (no.PD112)	£50-60
❏ AA32609	Avro Lancaster - 617 Squadron (no.PD113)	£50-60
❏ AA32611	Avro Lancaster - 97 Squadron	£88
❏ AA32612	Avro Lancaster - Guy Gibson	£92
❏ AA32613	Avro Lancaster - RAF Cornwall (1956)	£86
❏ AA32701	Hawker Hunter - Blue Diamonds	£20-25
❏ AA32702	Hawker Hunter - 1st Squadron RAF Brawdy (Ltd Ed 4000)	£20-25
❏ AA32703	Hawker Hunter - Boscombe Down	£20-25
❏ AA32704	Hawker Hunter - 43rd Squadron RAF Zerstoregeschwader 1	£20-25
❏ AA32705	Hawker Hunter - Rough Diamonds	£20-25
❏ AA32706	Hawker Hunter - Belgium Air Force	£20-25
❏ AA32707	Hawker Hunter - No.4 Squadron	£20-25
❏ AA32708	Hawker Hunter - La Patrouille Suisse	£20-25
❏ AA32709	Hawker Hunter - 12th Squadron	£20-25
❏ AA32710	Hawker Hunter - Swiss livery (non-aerobatic)	£20-25
❏ AA32711	Hawker Hunter - No.1 Squadron	£20-25
❏ AA32801	De Havilland Mosquito - Grim Reaper	£69
❏ AA32802	De Havilland Mosquito - 2nd TAF	£96
❏ AA32803	De Havilland Mosquito - NFII	£50-60

	Ref.	Model	Price Guide
❑	AA32804	De Havilland Mosquito - BOAC	£132
❑	AA32805	De Havilland Mosquito - 248 Squadron	£30-35
❑	AA32806	De Havilland Mosquito - 211 Squadron	£30-35
❑	AA32807	De Havilland Mosquito - USAAF	£30-35
❑	AA32808	De Havilland Mosquito - CAACU, Exeter	£33
❑	AA32809	De Havilland Mosquito - 235 Squadron	£38
❑	AA32810	De Havilland Mosquito - F for Freddie	£30-35
❑	AA32811	De Havilland Mosquito - TMk3	£30-35
❑	AA32812	De Havilland Mosquito - NFMk2	£30-35
❑	AA32813	De Havilland Mosquito - Harbour bombing raid	£30-35
❑	AA32814	De Havilland Mosquito - RAF Benson	£30-35
❑	AA32815	De Havilland Mosquito - HC Kelsey	£30-35
❑	AA32913	Boeing E3B - USAF AWACS	£40-50
❑	AA33001	Corsair F4U1A - White 7	£15-20
❑	AA33002	Corsair F4U1A - White 29	£33
❑	AA33003	Corsair F4U1A - 1835 Squadron	£29
❑	AA33004	Corsair F4U1A - Lucybelle	£15-20
❑	AA33005	Corsair F4U1A - White 167	£15-20
❑	AA33006	Corsair F4U1A - 1850 Squadron (Ltd Ed 2700)	£15-20
❑	AA33007	Corsair F4U1A - White 3	£15-20
❑	AA33008	Corsair F4U1A - White 576 Marines Dream	£15-20
❑	AA33009	Corsair F4U1A - 530	£15-20
❑	AA33010	Corsair F4U1A - Suez Campaign	£15-20
❑	AA33012	Corsair F4U1A - Jesse Folmar	£15-20
❑	AA33101	Mitsubishi - Hiryu	£31
❑	AA33102	Mitsubishi - Kokutai	£15-20
❑	AA33103	Mitsubishi - Zero Tainan	£15-20
❑	AA33104	Mitsubishi - Kasamigaura Flying Group	£15-20
❑	AA33105	Mitsubishi - Takeo Okumura	£24
❑	AA33201	McDonnell Phantom - Sundowners Squadron (Ltd Ed 1300)	£32
❑	AA33202	McDonnell Phantom - 74th Squadron	£25-35
❑	AA33203	McDonnell Phantom - Blue Angels	£25-35
❑	AA33204	McDonnell Phantom - USAF 12 TFTW	£25-35
❑	AA33205	McDonnell Phantom - Black Bunny	£25-35
❑	AA33206	McDonnell Phantom - VX-4 Squadron	£25-35
❑	AA33207	McDonnell Phantom - USMC VM FA531	£25-35
❑	AA33208	McDonnell Phantom - US Naval Missile Center	£25-35
❑	AA33209	McDonnell Phantom - Blue Angels	£25-35
❑	AA33210	McDonnell Phantom - 74th Squadron	£25-35
❑	AA33211	McDonnell Phantom - 171st Squadron	£25-35
❑	AA33212	McDonnell Phantom - VF-74 Squadron	£25-35
❑	AA33301	Boeing B17 - Memphis Belle	£85
❑	AA33302	Boeing B17 - Sweet & Lovely	£43
❑	AA33303	Boeing B17 - 220 Squadron	£74
❑	AA33304	Boeing B17 - Yankee Doodle	£40-50
❑	AA33305	Boeing B17 - 2nd Patches	£40-50
❑	AA33307	Boeing B17 - Confederate Air Force	£40-50
❑	AA33310	Boeing B17 - Zoot Suiters	£40-50
❑	AA33312	Boeing B17 - USAAF	£23
❑	AA33401	Westland Sea King Helicopter - 825 Squadron	£33
❑	AA33402	Sikorsky	£30-35
❑	AA33403	Sikorsky - US Presidential Flight	£37
❑	AA33404	Westland Sea King Helicopter - RAF Sea Rescue	£25-35
❑	AA33405	Sikorsky - US Marine Corps	£25-35
❑	AA33406	Westland Sea King Helicopter - 717 Squadron	£25-35
❑	AA33407	Westland Sea King Helicopter - Royal Australian Navy	£25-35
❑	AA33408	Sikorsky - HS3 US Navy Squadron	£25-35
❑	AA33410	Westland Sea King Helicopter - 824 Squadron	£25-35
❑	AA33413	Westland Sea King Helicopter - 814 Squadron	£25-35

Ref.	Model	Price Guide
❏ AA33414	Westland Sea King Helicopter - Falklands (1990)	£25-35
❏ AA33601	Panavia Tornado - RAF Honington (unlimited)	£18
❏ AA33602	Panavia Tornado - Gulf War	£22-27
❏ AA33603	Panavia Tornado - Royal Aircraft Establishment, Bedford	£22-27
❏ AA33604	Panavia Tornado - 27 Squadron	£22-27
❏ AA33605	Panavia Tornado - Tiger Meet	£22-27
❏ AA33606	Panavia Tornado - No.2 Squadron	£22-27
❏ AA33607	Panavia Tornado - Dambusters	£22-27
❏ AA33608	Panavia Tornado - German Navy	£22-27
❏ AA33609	Panavia Tornado - 12th Squadron	£22-27
❏ AA33701	Heinkel HE111 - Hindenburg	£66
❏ AA33702	Heinkel HE111 - Kuhlmey (Ltd Ed 3600)	£42
❏ AA33703	Heinkel HE111 - Kampfgeschwader 5S (Ltd Ed 3000)	£55
❏ AA33704	Heinkel HE111 - Ottana, Sardinia	£62
❏ AA33705	Heinkel HE111 - Russia (1943)	£65
❏ AA33706	Heinkel HE111 - KG26	£50-60
❏ AA33707	Heinkel HE111 - KG3	£50-60
❏ AA33708	Heinkel HE111 - StG3	£50-60
❏ AA33709	Heinkel HE111 - Blitz Bomber	£63
❏ AA33801	Thunderbolt P47D - Dave Schilling	£15-20
❏ AA33802	Thunderbolt P47D - 79 Squadron	£15-20
❏ AA33803	Thunderbolt P47D - USAF Miss Mary Lou	£15-20
❏ AA33804	Thunderbolt P47D - 11	£15-20
❏ AA33805	Thunderbolt P47D - Bonnie	£15-20
❏ AA33806	Thunderbolt P47D - No Guts No Glory	£15-20
❏ AA33808	Thunderbolt P47D - Harriet	£15-20
❏ AA33809	Thunderbolt P47D - Rozzie Geth	£15-20
❏ AA33812	Thunderbolt P47D - Darling Dottie 3	£15-20
❏ AA34001	Boeing B24 Liberator - The Dragon & His Tail	£67
❏ AA34002	Boeing B24 Liberator - Ball of Fire 3 (Ltd Ed 4400)	£80
❏ AA34003	Consolidated B24D Liberator - Strawberry Bitch	£50-60
❏ AA34004	Consolidated B24D Liberator - Sky Witch	£50-60
❏ AA34005	Consolidated B24D Liberator - 120th Squadron	£50-60
❏ AA34006	Consolidated B24D Liberator - Booby Trap	£50-60
❏ AA34007	Consolidated B24D Liberator - You Can't Miss It	£50-60
❏ AA34009	Consolidated B24D Liberator - 215 Squadron	£50-60
❏ AA34010	Consolidated B24D Liberator - Pistol Packin Mama	£50-60
❏ AA34012	Consolidated B24D Liberator - 223 Bomber Support Squadron	£72
❏ AA34015	Consolidated B24D Liberator - USAAF	£93
❏ AA34101	Blackburn Buccaneer - 809 Squadron	£20-25
❏ AA34102	Hawker Siddeley Buccaneer - 12 Squadron	£20-25
❏ AA34103	Blackburn Buccaneer - 801 Squadron	£20-25
❏ AA34104	Hawker Siddeley Buccaneer - 12 Squadron	£20-25
❏ AA34105	Hawker Siddeley Buccaneer - 208 Squadron	£20-25
❏ AA34106	Blackburn Buccaneer - 24 Squadron	£20-25
❏ AA34107	Hawker Siddeley Buccaneer - 15 Squadron	£20-25
❏ AA34108	Hawker Siddeley Buccaneer - Royal Aircraft Establishment, Bedford	£20-25
❏ AA34201	Chinook Helicopter - US Army	£31
❏ AA34202	Boeing Vertol Chinook Helicopter - 18 Squadron (Ltd Ed 5400)	£44
❏ AA34203	Boeing Vertol Chinook Helicopter - US Army (1961)	£25-30
❏ AA34204	Boeing Vertol Chinook Helicopter - Gulf War	£25-30
❏ AA34205	Boeing Vertol Chinook Helicopter - 12th Squadron	£25-30
❏ AA34207	Boeing Vertol Chinook Helicopter - BA	£25-30
❏ AA34208	Boeing Vertol Chinook Helicopter - BA	£25-30
❏ AA34209	Boeing Vertol Chinook Helicopter - Special Air Service Operations	£25-30
❏ AA34301	Focke-Wulf - White 8	£20-25
❏ AA34302	Focke-Wulf - Black Double Chevron	£20-25
❏ AA34303	Focke-Wulf - Hans Hahn	£20-25
❏ AA34304	Focke-Wulf - Adolf Dickfield	£20-25

Ref.	Model	Price Guide
❑ AA34305	Focke-Wulf - SG2 (Tunisia 1942)	£20-25
❑ AA34306	Focke-Wulf - Yellow 2	£20-25
❑ AA34307	Focke-Wulf - White 11	£20-25
❑ AA34310	Focke-Wulf - Captive Eagle	£20-25
❑ AA34701	English Electric Canberra - 10th Squadron	£46
❑ AA34702	Martin RB57A - 363 TRW	£17
❑ AA34703	English Electric Canberra - 98th Squadron	£30-40
❑ AA34704	Martin RB57A - 66 TRW	£30-40
❑ AA34705	English Electric Canberra - Air Atlantique	£30-40
❑ AA34706	English Electric Canberra - Boscombe Down	£30-40
❑ AA34707	English Electric Canberra - RNAS Yeovilton	£47
❑ AA34708	English Electric Canberra - 16th Squadron	£53
❑ AA34801	Vickers Wellington - 9th Squadron	£48
❑ AA34802	Vickers Wellington - 99th Squadron	£53
❑ AA34803	Vickers Wellington - 419 Squadron	£59
❑ AA34804	Vickers Wellington - 221 Squadron	£63
❑ AA34805	Vickers Wellington Chivenor	£60
❑ AA35001	Gloster Meteor - 500 Squadron	£20
❑ AA35002	Gloster Meteor - 601 Squadron	£20-25
❑ AA35003	Gloster Meteor - 1574 Flight	£20-25
❑ AA35004	Gloster Meteor - 77 Squadron	£20-25
❑ AA35005	Gloster Meteor - 208 Squadron	£20-25
❑ AA35006	Gloster Meteor - Dutch Air Force	£20-25
❑ AA35008	Gloster Meteor - 1st Squadron	£20-25
❑ AA35010	Gloster Meteor - 111st Squadron	£20-25
❑ AA35106	Lockheed - Trans Canada	£41
❑ AA35201	P40F Warhawk - Cpt John Bradley	£14
❑ AA35202	P40E Kittyhawk - Johnnie Gibson	£15-20
❑ AA35203	P40F Warhawk - White 86	£15-20
❑ AA35204	P40E Kittyhawk - 112 Squadron	£15-20
❑ AA35205	P40F Warhawk - Aletian Islands	£15-20
❑ AA35208	P40F Warhawk - Robert Scott	£15-20
❑ AA35211	P40F Warhawk - Typhoon McGoon	£15-20
❑ AA35214	P40F Warhawk - Robert Baseler (USSAF)	£15-20
❑ AA35301	B25 - Heavenly Body	£40-45
❑ AA35302	B25 - Doolittles Raider	£40-45
❑ AA35303	B25 - Bats Outa Hell	£40-45
❑ AA35304	B25 - 226 Squadron	£40-45
❑ AA35306	B25 - Black 110	£40-45
❑ AA35308	B25 - 345th Brigade	£40-45
❑ AA35309	B25 - 180th Squadron	£55
❑ AA35110	B25 - Legal Eagle	£55
❑ AA35401	SEPECAT Jaguar - 6th Squadron	£40
❑ AA35402	SEPECAT Jaguar - Gulf War	£35-45
❑ AA35403	SEPECAT Jaguar - 16th Squadron	£35-45
❑ AA35404	SEPECAT Jaguar - 54th Squadron	£35-45
❑ AA35405	SEPECAT Jaguar - 41st Squadron (RAF)	£35-45
❑ AA35408	SEPECAT Jaguar - 41st Squadron	£35-45
❑ AA35409	SEPECAT Jaguar - Boscombe Down	£35-45
❑ AA35603	Nimrod Mk1 - prototype	£20-25
❑ AA35701	ME262A - Adolf Galland	£15-20
❑ AA35702	ME262A - Yellow 5	£15-20
❑ AA35703	ME262A - Heinz Bar	£15-20
❑ AA35706	ME262A - Walter Nowotny	£15-20
❑ AA35801	F86 Sabre - Major Glen	£20-25
❑ AA35802	F86 Sabre - Shepherds Grove	£20-25
❑ AA35805	F86 Sabre - 93rd Squadron	£20-25
❑ AA35806	F86 Sabre - Royal Canadian Air Force	£20-25
❑ AA35812	F86 Sabre - TAF	£20-25

Ref.	Model	Price Guide
❏ AA35813	F86 Sabre - RAF Germany (1954)	£20-25
❏ AA35815	F86 Sabre - USAFE	£20-25
❏ AA35901	Blackhawk - USAF	£20-25
❏ AA35903	Jayhawk - US Coastguard	£20-25
❏ AA35904	Seahawk - Royal Australian Navy	£20-25
❏ AA35905	Desert Hawk - US Army	£20-25
❏ AA36001	BAE Hawk - Red Arrows	£20-25
❏ AA36002	BAE Hawk - Training School	£20-25
❏ AA36003	BAE Hawk - 208 Squadron	£20-25
❏ AA36004	McConnell Douglas Goshawk - prototype	£20-25
❏ AA36005	BAE Hawk - RAF Chivenor	£20-25
❏ AA36006	BAE Hawk - Training School	£20-25
❏ AA36101	Catalina - 209 Squadron	£73
❏ AA36102	Catalina - Emergency Rescue	£60-70
❏ AA36103	Catalina - RAF Sullom Voe	£60-70
❏ AA36104	Catalina - Black Cat	£55-65
❏ AA36105	Catalina Vickers - USAF	£55-65
❏ AA36106	Catalina - 205 Squadron	£55-65
❏ AA36201	Gloster Gladiator - 263 Squadron	£38
❏ AA36202	Gloster Gladiator - JW Sleigh	£30-35
❏ AA36203	Gloster Gladiator - Hal Far Fighter Flight	£30-35
❏ AA36204	Gloster Gladiator	£30-35
❏ AA36205	Gloster Gladiator - Peter Wykeham Barnes	£30-35
❏ AA36206	Gloster Gladiator - 6th Squadron	£30-35
❏ AA36301	Fairey Swordfish - 810 Squadron	£65
❏ AA36302	Fairey Swordfish - 810 Squadron	£34
❏ AA36303	Fairey Swordfish - 701 Catapult Flight	£47
❏ AA36304	Fairey Swordfish - Bircham Newton	£30-40
❏ AA36305	Fairey Swordfish - Fleet Air Arm	£30-40
❏ AA36306	Fairey Swordfish - Fleet Air Arm	£30-40
❏ AA36401	Eurofighter Typhoon - 17 Squadron	£31
❏ AA36402	Eurofighter Typhoon - 29 Squadron	£36
❏ AA36403	Eurofighter Typhoon - RAF Leuchars	£29
❏ AA36501	Hawker Typhoon - 451 Squadron	£17
❏ AA36502	Hawker Typhoon - 609 Squadron	£20-25
❏ AA36503	Hawker Typhoon - RAF Germany (1945)	£20-25
❏ AA36504	Hawker Typhoon - Butch Taylor	£20-25
❏ AA36505	Hawker Typhoon - Boscombe Down	£20-25
❏ AA36601	Locheed Lightning - Richard Bong (Ltd Ed 3990)	£20-25
❏ AA36602	Locheed Lightning - Eze Does It	£20-25
❏ AA36606	Locheed Lightning - Australian Air Force	£40-50
❏ AA36607	Locheed Lightning - Pat III	£40-50
❏ AA36608	Locheed Lightning - H Sealy	£40-50
❏ AA36701	Junkers JU88A - Crete	£34
❏ AA36702	Junkers JU88A - Adler Geschwader	£40-50
❏ AA36703	Junkers JU88A - Lister (Ltd Ed 2190)	£70
❏ AA36704	Junkers JU88A - Luftwaffe	£40-50
❏ AA36801	Westland Lysander - 225 Squadron	£29
❏ AA36802	Westland Lysander - 6th Squadron	£26
❏ AA36803	Westland Lysander - Western Desert	£15-20
❏ AA36804	Westland Lysander - 161 Squadron	£15-20
❏ AA36805	Westland Lysander - 13th Squadron	£32
❏ AA36899	Bare casting	£100
❏ AA36901	Junkers JU52 - Norway (Ltd Ed 1604)	£89
❏ AA36902	Junkers JU52 - Hungary (1944)	£60-70
❏ AA36903	Junkers JU52 - BA	£60-70
❏ AA36904	Junkers JU52 - Luftwaffe	£60-70
❏ AA37104	P51D Mustang - Tommy's Dad	£20-25
❏ AA37105	P51D Mustang - Algeria (1943)	£20-25

Ref.	Model	Price Guide
❏ AA37201	Halifax - 35th Squadron (Ltd Ed 2350)	£95
❏ AA37202	Halifax - Cyril Barton VC	£50-60
❏ AA37203	Halifax - Hormsley South (1943)	£50-60
❏ AA37301	De Havilland Vampire - Royal Auxillary Force	£19
❏ AA37302	De Havilland Vampire - 28th Squadron	£20-25
❏ AA37303	De Havilland Vampire - RAF Fassberg	£25-25
❏ AA37501	Mig29 - Vladimir Komarov	£27
❏ AA37601	Westland Wessex - 22nd Squadron	£35-45
❏ AA37602	Westland Wessex - South Atlantic (1982)	£35-45
❏ AA37603	Westland Wessex - RAF Odiham	£35-45
❏ AA37604	Sikorsky CH34 - US Army	£35-45
❏ AA38002	Fairchild Thunderbolt - USAF	£32

SETS

Ref.	Model	Price Guide
❏ AA39901	Falkland Harriers 2pce HMS Hermes diorama	£55
❏ AA99151	Suez Campaign 2pce set	£33
❏ AA99120	Guadalacanal 2pce set	£43
❏ AA99126	WW2 Pacific 3pce Set	£66
❏ AA99127	WW2 Blitz 3pce set	£67
❏ AA99133	Pathfinder 2pce set	£110
❏ AA99110	Reconnaisance 2pce set	£33
❏ AA99167	Chinook Helicopter & Land Rover 2pce set	£33
❏ AA99170	RAF No.1 Squadron 4pce set	£69
❏ AA99198	Johnnie Johnson Spitfires 3pce set	£69

1:48th SCALE

Ref.	Model	Price Guide
❏ 50401	Huey Hog Gunship	£25-30
❏ AA37701	SE5A - Home Defence	£25-30
❏ AA37702	SE5A - Billy Bishop	£25-30
❏ AA37801	Albatross - German Air Force	£25-30
❏ AA37802	Albatross - Von Roth	£25-30
❏ AA37901	Spad XIII - French Air Force	£25-30
❏ AA37902	Spad XIIIC1 - French Air Force	£25-30
❏ AA50413	Bell Huey - Marine Aircraft Group	£25-30
❏ AA51209	Cobra - US Army	£25-30
❏ AA51907	Bell - Army Historic Aircraft Flight	£25-30

1:32 SCALE

Ref.	Model	Price Guide
❏ AA33901	Supermarine Spitfire Mk1A	£80-100
❏ AA33902	Supermarine Spitfire Mk2	£80-100
❏ AA33903	Supermarine Spitfire Mk2A	£80-100
❏ AA33904	Supermarine Spitfire Mk1 - Kiwi	£80-100
❏ AA33905	Supermarine Spitfire Mk1 - Brian Lane	£80-100
❏ AA33908	Supermarine Spitfire - prototype	£80-100
❏ AA34401	Mustang P51 - Stinger	£45
❏ AA34402	Mustang P51 - Old Crow	£40-50
❏ AA34403	Mustang P51 - Big Beautiful Doll	£45-55
❏ AA34404	Mustang P51 - Jumping Jacks	£45-55
❏ AA34406	Mustang P51 - Jersey Jerk	£89
❏ AA34501	Wilbur & Orville Wright Flyer	£15-20
❏ AA34503	Wright Flyer - Carolina (1903)	£15-20
❏ AA34601	Mosquito - Moncton Express	£145
❏ AA34602	Mosquito - 544 Squadron	£80-100
❏ AA34603	109 Squadron	£80-100
❏ AA34901	Messerschmitt Bf109G - Red 6	£80-100
❏ AA34902	Messerschmitt Bf109G - Black Chevron	£80-100
❏ AA34904	Messerschmitt Bf109G - Eric Hartmann	£80-100
❏ AA34905	Messerschmitt Bf109G - Jagdivision	£80-100
❏ AA34906	Messerschmitt Bf109G - Heinrich Ehrle	£60-70
❏ AA34908	Messerschmitt Bf109G - Hermann Graf	£78

Ref.	Model	Price Guide
❑ AA35501	Hawker Hurricane - 249th Squadron	£70-80
❑ AA35502	Hawker Hurricane - AOC Malta	£61
❑ AA35504	Hawker Hurricane - 880 Squadron	£82
❑ AA35505	Hawker Hurricane - 242nd Squadron	£70-80
❑ AA35506	Hawker Hurricane	£70-80
❑ AA35507	Hawker Hurricane - 17th Squadron	£70-80

WARBIRDS 1:72 SCALE

❑ WB99601	Supermarine Spitfire - George Unwin	£10
❑ WB99602	Mustang P51 - E Horbaczewski	£10
❑ WB99603	Hawker Hurricane - Pete Brothers	£10
❑ WB99604	Messerschmitt - Helmut Wick	£10
❑ WB99805	Focke Wolf - Walter Nowotny	£10
❑ WB99606	Chance Vought Corsair - Ken Walsh	£10
❑ WB99607	Thunderbolt P47D - Dave Schilling	£10
❑ WB99608	Junkers Stuka - Ulrich Rudel	£10
❑ WB99609	Lancaster - Mickey the Moocher	£10
❑ WB99610	Kittyhawk - Les Jackson	£10
❑ WB99611	Mitsubishi Zero Sen - Nishizawa	£10
❑ WB99612	Flying Fortress - Sally B	£10
❑ WB99613	Messerschmitt - Heinz Bar	£10
❑ WB99614	Spitfire - Otto Smik	£10
❑ WB99615	Kittyhawk - Clive Tolhurst	£10
❑ WB99616	Mustang P51D - Hurry Home Honey	£10
❑ WB99617	Spitfire - Douglas Bader	£10
❑ WB99618	Messerschmitt - Luftwaffe	£10
❑ WB99619	Focke Wolf - Luftwaffe	£10
❑ WB99620	Hurricane - Bob Stanford Tuck	£10
❑ WB99621	Junkers JU87B - Luftwaffe	£10
❑ WB99622	Lancaster - City of Lincoln	£10
❑ WB99623	Mitsubishi - Japan Air Force	£10
❑ WB99624	P47D Thunderbolt - Pengie II	£10
❑ WB99625	Lightning P38J - Pudgie IV	£10
❑ WB99626	Corsair - Hammy Gray	£10
❑ WB99627	Flying Fortess - Give it to Uncle	£10
❑ WB99628	Typhoon - Denis Gilam	£10
❑ WB99629	Messerschmitt - Hermann Buchner	£10
❑ WB99630	Spitfire - George Beurling	£10

1:72 SCALE PREDATORS

❑ PR99401	Junkers Stuka - Luftwaffe	£10-15
❑ PR99402	Grumman Hellcat - US Navy	£10-15
❑ PR99403	Grumman Avenger - US Navy	£10-15
❑ PR99404	Mig21	£10-15
❑ PR99405	Douglas Duantless - US Navy	£10-15
❑ PR99406	Lockheed Starfighter - USAF	£10-15
❑ PR99407	Junkers Stuka - Luftwaffe	£10-15
❑ PR99408	Grumman Hellcat - US Navy	£10-15
❑ PR99409	Grumman Avenger - US Navy	£10-15
❑ PR99410	Mig21	£10-15
❑ PR99411	Douglas Duantless - US Navy	£10-15
❑ PR99412	Lockheed Starfighter -	£10-15
❑ PR99413	Junkers Stuka - Luftwaffe	£10-15
❑ PR99414	Grumman Hellcat	£10-15
❑ PR99415	Grumman Avenger	£10-15
❑ PR99416	Mig21 - Indian Air Force	£10-15
❑ PR99417	Douglas Duantless - US Navy	£10-15
❑ PR99418	Lockheed Starfighter - PAF	£10-15

US Issues

Ref.	Model	Price
❏ US31104	B17 Bomber - Memphis Belle	£15
❏ US31923	Spitfire - Debden, Essex	£14
❏ US32110	Messerschmitt - Audembert (1940)	£15-20
❏ US32213	Mustang P51K - Mrs Bonnie	£15
❏ US32214	Mustang P51K - Shu Shu	£15-20
❏ US32215	Mustang P51K - Creamers Dream	£15-20
❏ US32218	Mustang P51K - E Reghetti	£15-20
❏ US32221	Mustang P51K - Bud Mahurin	£15-20
❏ US32222	Mustang P51K - E McComas	£15-20
❏ US32225	Mustang P51K - Robin Olds	£15-20
❏ US32226	Mustang P51K - Gordon Graham	£15-20
❏ US32227	Mustang P51K - Sizzlin Liz	£15-20
❏ US32509	Junkers - Krainici	£15-20
❏ US33216	Phantom - Marine Corps	£15-20
❏ US33217	Phantom - USS Sarotoga	£15-20
❏ US33219	Phantom - Robin Olds	£15-20
❏ US33306	B17 - Bit O Lace	£83
❏ US33308	B17 - Mount N Ride	£79
❏ US33309	B17 - Nine O Nine	£102
❏ US33311	Flying Fortress - Italy	£90-110
❏ US33411	Sea King - Chink 69 (Ltd Ed 1600)	£39
❏ US33710	Heinkel - H Gabbert	£67
❏ US33811	P47D Thunderbolt - G Eagleton (Ltd Ed 2700)	£27
❏ US33813	P47D Thunderbolt - Tuskegee	£20-30
❏ US33815	P47D Thunderbolt - B Mahurin	£20-30
❏ US33816	P47D Thunderbolt - Miss Plainfield	£20-30
❏ US33817	P47D Thunderbolt - Edwin Fisher	£20-30
❏ US33818	P47D Thunderbolt - Katy Did	£20-30
❏ US33819	P47D Thunderbolt - Duane Beeson	£20-30
❏ US33821	P47D Thunderbolt - Raydon, Suffolk	£20-30
❏ US33906	Spitfire - G Unwin	£85
❏ US34011	Liberator - Michigan	£58
❏ US34014	Liberator - Sleepy Time Gal	£100
❏ US34206	Chinook - Guns a Go Go	£38
❏ US34308	Focke-Wulf - W Mowotny	£27
❏ US34405	Mustang - Old Crow	£77
❏ US34407	Mustang - John Elder	£74
❏ US34903	Messerschmitt- G Barkhorn	£79
❏ US35207	Kittyhawk - Australian Air Force	£20-30
❏ US33212	P40E - R Vaught	£20-30
❏ US35305	B25 - Oujda, Morocco	£67
❏ US35307	PBJ1J - Solomon Islands	£63
❏ US35503	Hurricane - 85th Squadron	£71
❏ US35705	Messerschmitt - Rudolph Sinner (Ltd Ed 2140)	£15
❏ US35804	F86E - W Mahurin	£20-30
❏ US35810	F86E - Ralph Parr	£20-30
❏ US36603	Lightning P38J - Robin Olds	£20-30
❏ US36604	Lightning P38J - Kings Cliffe (1944)	£20-30
❏ US37101	Mustang P51D - Missouri Mauler	£20-30
❏ US50401	Huey Helicopter - LA Fire Dept	£20-30
❏ US50402	Huey Frog Helicopter	£20-30
❏ US50403	Huey Frog Helicopter	£20-30
❏ US50405	Huey Frog - Medevac	£20-30
❏ US51202	Bell Cobra Helicopter	£20-30
❏ US51203	Bell Cobra Helicopter - Vietnam	£20-30
❏ US51206	Bell Cobra Helicopter - Florida Forestry Division	£20-30
❏ US51902	Bell Sioux Helicopter	£20-30

MILITARY

Ref.	Model	Range	Price Guide
7501	Land Rover Mk2 & trailer	Fighting Vehicles	£27
55101	Diamond T transporter & tank	Fighting Vehicles	£45
55601	Diamond T wrecker (Ltd Ed 10300)	Fighting Vehicles	£37
69901	Centurion tank & Saladin armoured vehicle	Fighting Vehicles	£76
69902	Bedford truck & gun	Fighting Vehicles	£30-35
69903	Tiger Mk1 tank	Fighting Vehicles	£27
CC51004	M4 A3 Sherman tank - British Army, Trowbridge (Ltd Ed 3100)	World War 2	£24
CC51005	M4 A2 Sherman tank - French	World War 2	£20-25
CC51006	M4 A3 Sherman tank - US	World War 2	£20-25
CC51007	M4 A2 Sherman tank - 9th Armoured Brigade	World War 2	£20-25
CC51015	M4 A4 Sherman tank - observation post	World War 2	£20-25
CC51016	M4 Sherman tank	World War 2	£20-25
CC51017	M4 A3 Sherman tank - Blockbuster	World War 2	£20-25
CC51025	M4 A3 Sherman tank - 341st Battallion	World War 2	£20-25
CC51602	T34 tank - 6th Corps	World War 2	£20-25
CC51707	Dodge Weapons Carrier - US	World War 2	£20-25
CC51708	WC56 Command Car - US	World War 2	£16
CC55107	Diamond T transporter (Ltd Ed 3500)	World War 2	£32
CC55108	Diamond T transporter & Sherman tank	World War 2	£72
CC60001	Sd.Kfz Krauss Maffei Semi Track & gun	World War 2	£27
CC60002	Sd.Kfz Krauss Maffei Semi Track - German 12th Army	World War 2	£20-25
CC60003	Sd.Kfz Krauss Maffei Semi Track - German Army	World War 2	£20-25
CC60004	Sd.Kfz Krauss Maffei Semi Track personnel carrier - Afrika Korps	World War 2	£20-25
CC60008	Krauss Maffei Half Track	World War 2	£20-25
CC60101	Churchill Mk3 tank - Canadian	World War 2	£17
CC60102	Churchill Mk4 tank - 5th Guard	World War 2	£20-25
CC60103	Churchill NA75 - British	World War 2	£20-25
CC60104	Churchill Mk3 tank - British (El Alamein)	World War 2	£20-25
CC60105	Churchill Mk3 tank - British (Tunisia)	World War 2	£20-25
CC60201	PzKpfw V Panther tank - Panzer Regmt.	World War 2	£21
CC60202	Panther tank - German Army	World War 2	£20-25
CC60203	PzKpfw V Panther tank - Panzer Regmt. (Eastern Front)	World War 2	£20-25
CC60207	Panther AUSF G tank	World War 2	£20-25
CC60208	Panther AUSF G tank	World War 2	£20-25
CC60301	Bedford Troop Carrier, Royal Navy	World War 2	NPA
CC60302	Bedford Command Signals vehicle - British Army	World War 2	£20-25
CC60303	Bedford supply truck - 7th Armoured	World War 2	£20-25
CC60306	Bedford wireless body	World War 2	£20-25
CC60405	M16 Quad Gun	World War 2	£20-25
CC60407	M3A1 Half Track	World War 2	£18
CC60411	M16 Multiple Gun motor carriage - US	World War 2	£20-25
CC60504	PZKPFW Tiger tank - AUSF E	World War 2	£20-25
CC60505	PZKPFW Tiger tank - AUSF E	World War 2	£20-25
CC60510	PZKPFW Tiger tank - Will Fay	World War 2	£20-25
CC60604	Cruiser tank Mk2	World War 2	£20-25
CC60605	Cruiser tank A34	World War 2	£20-25
CC60611	Cromwell tank diorama set	World War 2	£42
CC61106	Tiger & T34 2pce tank diorama set	World War 2	£68
CC51013	M4 A3 Sherman tank - Blockbuster	D-Day Landings	£15-20
CC60006	SDKFZ Krauss Maffei Semi Track & gun	D-Day Landings	£16
CC60107	Churchill Mk3 tank	D-Day Landings	£15-20
CC60108	Churchill Mk3 tank	D-Day Landings	£15-20
CC60206	Panther tank	D-Day Landings	£15-20
CC60305	Bedford QLD	D-Day Landings	£15-20
CC60402	M3A1 Half Track	D-Day Landings	£15-20
CC60404	M3 Half Track - white	D-Day Landings	£15-20

AEC Water Tender & Ladder Fire Engines.
Sold for £30 Toy Price Guide Archive

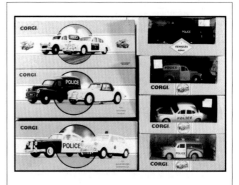

Corgi Classics police vehicles; 4 individual cars
& 3 sets. Sold for £65 DJ Auctions

Ref.	Model	Range	Price Guide
❏ US60501	Tiger tank - SS Panzer	D-Day Landings	£15-20
❏ CC60502	Tiger tank - 101st	D-Day Landings	£15-20
❏ CC60601	Cromwell tank	D-Day Landings	£15-20
❏ CC60603	Cruiser tank	D-Day Landings	£15-20
❏ US51010	M4 A3 Sherman tank - Thunderbolt	D-Day Landings	£15-20
❏ US51011	M4 A3 Sherman tank	D-Day Landings	£15-20
❏ US60005	SDKFZ Krauss Maffei Semi Track	D-Day Landings	£10-15
❏ US60204	Panther tank AUSF A	D-Day Landings	£15-20
❏ US60401	M341 Half Track	D-Day Landings	£10-15
❏ CC51020	M4 A3 Sherman tank - US	VE Day	£26
❏ CC60009	Krauss Maffei Personnel Carrier	VE Day	£15-20
❏ CC60210	PzKpfw Panther tank - Panzer Div.	VE Day	£36
❏ CC60410	M3 Half track - US	VE Day	£15-20
❏ CC60411	M16 Multiple Gun Motor Carriage - US	VE Day	£15-20
❏ CC60506	PzKpfw Tiger tank - Schwere Panzer	VE Day	£15-20
❏ CC60606	Cruiser tank A34 Comet - British 11th Armoured	VE Day	£15-20
❏ CC60607	Cruiser tank Mk2 - British 11th Armoured	VE Day	£15-20
❏ CC51028	Sherman tank - US, 3 figures	Skirmish	£28
❏ CC60011	SdLfz Anti Aircraft Gun - German Army	Skirmish	£19
❏ CC60109	Churchill tank - British	Skirmish	£27
❏ CC60213	Panther tank - German	Skirmish	£25-30
❏ CC60416	M16 Quad Half Track - US	Skirmish	£19
❏ CC60610	Cromwell Centaur tank - British	Skirmish	£24

Pair of Vintage Glory Steam Engines comprising Fowlers Showman's & B6 Road Engine.
Sold for £38 DJ Auctions

Ref.	Model	Range	Price Guide

STEAM VEHICLES 1:50 SCALE

Ref.	Model	Range	Price Guide
❏ 22402	Princess Royal Garrett 4CD on Bedford TK low loader		£36
❏ 80001	Tate & Lyle Super Sentinel		£21
❏ 80002	Paul Bros Ltd Sentinel		£18
❏ 80003	Shepherd Neame Ltd Sentinel		£23
❏ 80004	Wynn's Sentinel		£26
❏ 80005	Blue Circle Sentinel		£26
❏ 80006	McMullen Sentinel		£27
❏ 80007	United Africa Co Ltd Sentinel		£24
❏ 80008	Morris Co Sentinel		£20-25
❏ 80009	Charringtons Sentinel		£15-20
❏ 80010	Guinness Sentinel		£24
❏ 80101	Anderton & Rowlands Fowler Showmans		£62
❏ 80102	Pickfords Fowler Road Loco		£48
❏ 80103	Over the Sticks Fowler Showmans		£38
❏ 80104	Norman Box Fowler Road Loco		£27
❏ 80105	SJ Wharton Fowler Showmans		£40
❏ 80106	Eastnor Steam Haulage Co Fowler Road Loco		£29
❏ 80107	Silver plated Fowler Showmans		£29
❏ 80108	Wolverhampton Wanderer Fowler Crane		£36
❏ 80109	Fowler Road Engine War Dept		£33
❏ 80110	Circuit Mont Blanc Fowler Engine & Caravan		£52
❏ 80111	Super Lion Fowler Stump Cutter		£34
❏ 80112	Duke of York Fowler Engine		£33
❏ 80201	Tate & Lyle Foden		£36
❏ 80202	Bishop & Sons Foden		£21
❏ 80203	Ashworth & Sons Foden		£15-20
❏ 80204	Ind Coope Foden		£15-20
❏ 80205	Pickfords Foden		£15-20
❏ 80206	Guinness Foden		£15-20
❏ 80301	Bunty Garrett Road Tractor		£24
❏ 80302	Consuelo Allen Garrett Road Roller		£26
❏ 80303	Little Billy Garrett Showmans		£22
❏ 80304	The Baroness Garrett Road Roller		£19
❏ 80305	Wynns Garrett Road Tractor		£37
❏ 80306	Lord George Garrett Showmans		£28
❏ 80307	Victor Garrett Road Tractor		£38
❏ 80308	Princess Maud Garrett Showmans		£28
❏ 80309	Mr Potter Garrett Road Tractor		£16
❏ CC20001	Tarmac Sentinel	Dibnah's Choice	£16
❏ CC20002	Express Dairies Sentinel	Vintage Glory	£16

Trio of Vintage Glory Sentinel Platform
Wagons; United Africa, Morris's & Homepride.
Sold for £35 DJ Auctions

Trio of Vintage Glory Fowler B6's; Super Lion, The
Lion 7 Crane Engine. Sold for £95 DJ Auctions

Ref.	Model	Range	Price Guide
❏ CC20003	Johnson & Co Sentinel	Vintage Glory	£15
❏ CC20004	EC Gransen Sentinel	Vintage Glory	£18
❏ CC20101	Norman Box Fowler Road Loco	Dibnah's Choice	£37
❏ CC20102	Deakin & Sons Fowler Showmans	Vintage Glory	£28-35
❏ CC20105	King Carnival II Fowler Showmans (Ltd Ed 2000)	Vintage Glory	£37
❏ CC20107	John Murphy Fowler (Ltd Ed 2000)	Gold Star	£28-35
❏ CC20108	McGivens Fowler Showmans	Vintage Glory	£28-35
❏ CC20109	Anderton & Rowlands Jungle Ride Fowler Showmans	Vintage Glory	£42
❏ CC20110	Sir John Fowler Fowler Showmans		£28-35
❏ CC21006	Lightning Swirl Fowler Showmans		£28-35
❏ CC20201	Newquay Steam Foden		£28-35
❏ CC20202	Openshaw Brewery Foden	Dibnah's Choice	£28-35
❏ CC20203	Anglo American Oil Foden		£28-35
❏ CC20204	GWR Foden		£28-35
❏ CC20205	Fullers Foden		£28-35
❏ CC20206	WJ King Foden		£28-35
❏ CC20301	The Mighty Atom Garrett Showmans	Dibnah's Choice	£19
❏ CC20302	War Dept Garrett (Ltd Ed 2000)	Vintage Glory	£38
❏ CC20304	Pride of the South Garrett Showmans	Gold Star	£28-35
❏ CC20305	Katrina Garrett Showmans	Vintage Glory	£19
❏ CC20308	Adventurer Garrett		£20-25
❏ CC20501	Duke of Kent Burrell Road Loco		£40-50
❏ CC20503	Anderton & Rowlands Burrell Loco & organ		£40-50
❏ CC20504	Dragon Burrell Showmans		£40-50
❏ CC20505	Nero Burrell Showmans		£40-50

Chipperfields Circus Foden Closed Pole Truck with Caravan, AEC Cage Truck & Caravan & Booking Vehicle. Sold for £82 Toy Price Guide Archive

D949/17 Bedford OB Coach, Corgi Classics Special livery in grey box.
Sold for £9 Toy Price Guide Archive

Ref.	Model	Price Guide

CIRCUS, SHOWMAN'S & FAIRGROUND

Chipperfields (1:43 Scale)

❏	7202	Public Address Land Rover with clown figures (Ltd Ed 11500)	£20
❏	11201	ERF KV Trailer with cages & tigers	£37
❏	14201	Foden S21 Trailer & Tank with crocodile & hippo figures	£37
❏	17801	Scammel Cannon with ringmaster figure	£27
❏	31703	Chipperfields 4pce set	£50
❏	31901	Liberty Horses	£23
❏	31902	Foden S21 Trailer & Tank with elephants	£38
❏	96905	Bedford CA van booking office	£17
❏	97022	AEC Regal Coach	£33
❏	97092	Bedford Pantechnicon, Bertie Smee wardrobe	£29
❏	97303	Bedford Artic	£75
❏	97885	Scammell Highwayman, caravan & pole trailer	£55
❏	97886	Scammel Crane Truck	£21
❏	97887	Bedford artic & horsebox	£32
❏	97888	Pole Truck & Caravan	£39
❏	97889	AEC Truck & Cages	£36
❏	97896	AEC Pole Truck	£50
❏	97915	Scammell Highwayman & 2 trailers	£36
❏	97957	ERF 8-Wheeler	£42
❏	-	1995 Chipperfields Calendar	£12
❏	-	Figures 1st series	£10
❏	-	Figures 2nd series	£10

Billy Smarts

❏	97300	Bedford O Articulated	£24
❏	97891	AEC Mercury Truck & Trailer (Ltd Ed 6300)	£24
❏	97897	Scammell Highwayman, trailer & pole truck	£31
❏	CC02001	Mini van	£9

Jean Richard Pinder (FRENCH SERIES)

❏	7201	Land Rover loudspeaker van	£13-18
❏	16801	Scammell with gorilla & polar bear cages	£50
❏	35202	Daimler double decker bus	£13-18
❏	55401	Diamond T980	£27
❏	70101	Berliet elephant van	£30-35
❏	70201	Berliet canon	£30-35
❏	70301	Berliet horse transporter	£30-35
❏	70401	Berliet breakdown truck	£30-35
❏	70502	Renault 1000KG van	£13-18

TY88809 ERF Fuel Tanker, JET livery in blue
Superhaulers box.
Sold for £15 Toy Price Guide Archive

59511 Volvo Curtainside, KIT KAT livery in grey
Superhaulers box.
Sold for £12 Toy Price Guide Archive

Ref.	Model	Price Guide
❏ 70509	Renault 1000KG van - Spectactle Nouveau	£13-18
❏ 70609	Peugeot D3A - Fred Adison Orchestra	£13-18
❏ 71202	Renault tanker	£20-25
❏ 71402	Renault Cuisine van	£20-25
❏ 71901	Renault JL20 van - Podium	£20-25
❏ 72004	Bernard van	£20-25
❏ 72802	UNIC Saverne van	£20-25
❏ 72906	Simca lion & gibbon van	£20-25
❏ 72912	Simca tiger van	£20-25
❏ 73301	Berliet van - Super Cirque	£48
❏ 73401	Berliet van & trailer	£20-25
❏ 74301	Citroen dropside & trailer	£20-25
❏ EX11402	Bedford kangeroo truck & trailer	£20-25
❏ EX11404	Bedford kitchen trailer	£20-25
❏ EX51704	Dodge grizzly bear trailer	£20-25
❏ EX51705	Dodge - Visit the Zoo	£20-25
❏ EX70002	Berliet artic	£20-25
❏ EX70003	Berliet sleeping trailer	£20-25
❏ EX70528	Renault 1000KG - Pinder ORTF	£13-18
❏ EX70626	Peugeot publicity vehicle	£13-18
❏ EX70907	Saviem animal transporter	£30-35
❏ EX70908	Saviem refrigerated vehicle	£30-35
❏ EX72915	Simca van - Pinder on Ice	£13-18
❏ EX72917	Simca van & trailer	£30-35
❏ EX72918	Simca transporter	£30-35
❏ EX72919	Simca - Confiserie	£30-35

Other Circus

❏ 97083	Bedford Pantechnicon (Blackpool)	£15
❏ 97892	AEC Eergonomic truck & trailer (Houseman)	£24
❏ 97893	AEC Mercury & trailer (Ayers Ltd Ed 5900)	£23
❏ CC12303	Scammell Contractor (Austin Bros)	£24
❏ CC12606	Scammell Crusader (Robert Bros)	£34

Showmans Range

❏ 6601	Carters Morris Minor van	£10
❏ 7413	Biddalls Land Rover & horse	£20
❏ 9901	Collins ERF dodgem truck & trailer	£33
❏ 12601	Silcocks foden	£25
❏ 14101	Tuby's Foden truck & trailer	£30
❏ 15901	Anderton & Rowland Scammell & dodgem trailer	£43

CC13516 Volvo FM Curtainside, 2060 Limited Edition Countrywide Farmers livery (2006 issue). Sold for £19 Toy Price Guide Archive

31007 Annis & Co Ltd Diamond T Ballast & Locomotive load, 9400 Limited Edition (1997 issue). Sold for £72 Toy Price Guide Archive

Ref.	Model	Price Guide
❏ 16101	John Crow Scammell crane	£20
❏ 16501	Carters Scammell, trailer & caravan	£38
❏ 16502	Collins Scammell, trailer & caravan	£38
❏ 16602	Jennings Scammell & dodgem trailer	£38
❏ 21701	John Cordona AEC &Pole truck	£33
❏ 24401	John Cordona Leyland flatbed	£25
❏ 24801	Silcocks Leyland dodgen truck & caravan	£33
❏ 27602	Billy Crow Atkinson & trailer	£31
❏ 27801	Anderton & Rowland Atkinson pole truck	£22
❏ 31012	Mickey Kiely Foden with caravan, boxing ring & figures	£55
❏ 31702	Sadlers Fun Fair 3pce Set	£33
❏ 55609	Thurstons Amusements Diamond T with generator load	£41
❏ CC11911	Anderton & Rowland ERF (Ltd Ed 2300)	£28
❏ CC12423	Wilsons Dodgems Volvo Globetrotter & trailer	£43
❏ CC12425	Mannings Volvo Globetrotter	£49

Fairground Attractions

❏ CC07401	Harris's Gallopers Land Rover & trailer	£34
❏ CC10203	Carters Swingboats ERF (Ltd Ed 4000)	£39
❏ CC10303	Harris's AEC	£40
❏ CC10705	AEC Scammell & caravan	£38
❏ CC10706	Carters Scammell box trailer	£48
❏ CC10802	Harris's Foden S21	£38
❏ CC10804	Carters Foden S21	£48
❏ CC11506	Carters AEC MkV & caravan	£50
❏ CC20103	Harris's Fowler Showman	£38
❏ CC20104	Carter's Fowler Showman (Ltd Ed 2000)	£31
❏ CC20303	F Harris & Sons Garrett Showman	£24
❏ CC20401	Galloper	£75
❏ CC20402	Carters Steam Gallopers	£70
❏ CC20403	Anderton & Rowlands Steam Gallopers	£28-35
❏ CC55104	Harris's Diamond T with generator load	£37

4 James Bond cars including Aston Martin DB5,
Lotus Esprit, Toyota 2000 & Citroen 2CV.
Sold for £35 DJ Auctions

3 James Bond Collection 007 models each
including figure comprising; DB5, Toyota 2000 &
Lotus Esprit. Sold for £65 DJ Auctions

Ref.	Model	Price Guide

TV, FILM & CHARACTER MODELS

James Bond 007

❏ 4201	Gold Aston Martin DB5, Oddjob figure	£17
❏ 4202	Gold plated Aston Martin DB5 - Goldfinger 35th Anniversary	£32
❏ 4301	Silver Aston Martin DB5 - Goldeneye	£17
❏ 4302	Silver Aston Martin DB5	£10
❏ 4303	Silver Aston Martin DB5	£10
❏ 4303	Silver Aston Martin DB5 (Collect 1999 Show issue)	£27
❏ 65001	Lotus Esprit, Jaws figure	£15
❏ 65101	Toyota 2000GT, Blofeld figure	£15
❏ 65102	Toyota 2000GT, You Only Live Twice version with rear firing light	£15
❏ 65201	Moon Buggy	£15
❏ 65301	Citroen 2CV, James Bond figure	£15
❏ 65401	Space Shuttle, hugo Drax figure	£14
❏ 65501	Stromberg Helicopter, Naomi figure	£15
❏ 92978	Ferrari 355, Goldeneye	£18
❏ 96445	Gold plated Aston Martin, 30th Anniversary model	£38
❏ 96655	Silver Aston Martin (1:43 scale)	£15
❏ 96656	Gold Aston Martin (1:43 scale)	£15
❏ 96657	Aston Martin, Goldeneye (1:36 scale)	£15
❏ CC04001	Space Shuttle, Moonraker	£8
❏ CC04101	Stromberg Helicopter,The Spy Who Loved Me	£9
❏ CC04401	Moonbuggy, Diamonds Are Forever	£12

1:64 Scale (mounted on blister cards)

❏ 99651	Sunbeam Alpine, Dr No	£3-5
❏ 99652	Aston Martin DB5, Thunderball	£6
❏ 99653	Ford Mustang, Goldfinger	£3-5
❏ 99654	Toyota 2000GT, You Only Live Twice	£3-5
❏ 99655	Mercury Cougar, On Her Majesty's Secret Service	£3-5
❏ 99657	Lotus Esprit, The Spy Who Loved Me	£3-5
❏ 99658	Aston Martin DB7, The Living Daylights	£3-5
❏ 99659	Aston Martin DB5 - Goldeneye	£3-5
❏ 99662	Lotus Esprit, For Your Eyes Only	£3-5
❏ 99725	Ford Mustang, Diamonds are Forever	£3-5
❏ CC06101	Double Decker, Live & Let Die Double	£3-5

1:36th Scale

❏ 2101	Mustang Mach 1, Diamonds are Forever	£6
❏ 4304	Aston Martin DB5, Goldfinger	£6-8
❏ 4601	Gyrocopter, You Only Live Twice	£6-8

94060 James Bond Aston Martin,
silver with red interior, gold bumpers
& silver hubs.
Sold for £40 DJ Auctions

Corgi for Marks & Spencer 1:36 scale DB5
with leather keyring, silver with black interior.
Sold for £38 DJ Auctions

Ref.	Model	Price Guide
4701	Lotus Esprit Turbo, For your Eyes Only	£6-8
4801	Aston Matin V8, Living Daylights	£6-8
4901	BMW Z3, Goldeneye	£6-8
5001	BMW Z8, The World Is Not Enough	£6-8
5101	BMW 750i, Tomorrow Never Dies	£6-8
65102	Toyota 2000GT, You Only Live Twice	£6-8
5701	Mercedes, Octopussy	£6-8
6305	Aston Matin DB5, Goldfinger	£6-8
65002	Lotus Esprit, The Spy Who Loved Me	£6-8
CC04306	Aston Martin DB5 (including figures)	£6-8
CC4307	Gold plated Aston Martin	£16
CC4401	Moonbuggy, Diamonds Are Forever	£6-8
CC04512	Underwater Lotus Esprit	£6-8
CC04602	Gyrocopter, James Bond figure	£6-8
CC04704	Lotus Turbo	£6-8
CC04904	BMW Z3 (including figures)	£6-8
CC05004	BMW Z8	£6-8
CC05014	BMW 750i	£6-8
CC06101	Double Decker Bus, Live & Let Die	£6-8
CC06401	Renault Taxi, View To A Kill	£6-8
CC06803	Rolls Royce, Oddjob figure	£6-8
CC07503	Aston Martin V12 Vanquish, Die Another Day	£6-8
CC07505	Gold plated Aston Martin V12 Vanquish	£19
CC07603	Jaguar XKR, Zao figure, Die Another Day	£9
CC85701	Citroen 2CV, For your Eyes Only	£9-12
CC99105	BMW Z8, The World Is Not Enough	£15
CC99106	007 4pce Film Cannister set	£27
CC99171	2pce Gold plated Aston Martin DBS & V12 Vanquish set	£35

ULTIMATE BOND COLLECTION (later issues in blue window box with header card)

TY02102	Mustang Mach 1	£5-10
TY02501	Sunbeam Alpine	£11
TY04510	Underwater Lotus Esprit	£5-10
TY04702	Lotus Esprit Turbo	£8
TY04802	Aston Martin V8	£5-10
TY04902	BMW Z3	£5-10
TY05002	BMW Z8	£5-10
TY05012	BMW 750i	£5-10
TY05202	Toyota 2000GT	£5-10
TY05702	Mercedes	£5-10
TY06102	Double Decker Bus	£7
TY06402	Renault Taxi	£5-10

04202 35th Anniversary James Bond Goldfinger
Aston Martin, gold with red interior.
Sold for £25 DJ Auctions

96656 Special Edition James Bond Aston Martin,
gold with red interior. Sold for £20 DJ Auctions

Ref.	Model	Price Guide
☐ TY064701	Chevrolet Truck	£5-10
☐ TY06801	Rolls Royce	£5-10
☐ TY06901	Aston Martin DB5	£5-10
☐ TY07001	Aston Martin DB5	£5-10
☐ TY07101	AMC Hornet Hatchback, The Man With The Golden Gun	£8
☐ TY07201	Kenworth Tanker, Licensed To Kill	£5-10
☐ TY07501	Aston Martin Vanquish	£5-10
☐ TY04702	Space Shuttle	£5-10
☐ TY95101	Little Nellie	£5-10
☐ TY95201	Aston Martin Vanquish	£5-10
☐ TY95301	Aston Martin DB5	£5-10
☐ TY95401	Jaguar XKR	£5-10
☐ TY95501	BMW Z3	£5-10
☐ TY95601	Rolls Royce Sedanca de Ville	£5-10
☐ TY95701	Underwater Lotus Esprit	£5-10
☐ TY95801	Space Shuttle	£5-10
☐ TY95901	2pce Aston Martin Vanquish & Jaguar XKR set, James Bond & Zao figures	£14
☐ TY95902	2pce Aston Martin DB5 & Rolls Royce set, James Bond & Oddjob figures	£16
☐ TY93994	2pce Casino Royale DB5 set	NPA
	Batman	
☐ US77301	Batmobile (1960s styling)	£5-10
☐ US77302	Batmobile (2004 styling)	£5-10
☐ US77303	Batmobile (1990 styling)	£5-10
☐ US77304	Jokermobile (1950s styling)	£5-10
☐ US77305	Batmarine (1970s styling)	£5-10
☐ US77307	Batmobile (1980s styling)	£5-10
☐ US77308	Batmobile (2003 styling)	£5-10
☐ US77309	Batmobile (1940s styling)	£5-10
☐ US77310	Silver Age Collection set (1960s styling)	£5-10
☐ US77312	Batman 4pce set	£25
☐ US77314	Batmobile (1950s styling) 1:43	£5-10
☐ US77315	Batmobile (1970s styling) 1:43	£5-10
☐ US77316	Batmobile 2nd version (1990s styling) 1:43	£5-10
☐ US77517	Batmobile Roadster (1940s styling)	£5-10
☐ US77318	Facecar (1950s styling)	£5-10
☐ US77319	Robin Redbird car 1:43	£32
☐ US77320	Batmobile Convertible (1960s styling)	£5-10
☐ US77321	Bat Submersible (2000 styling)	£5-10
☐ US77322	Catmobile	£5-10
☐ US77323	Batmobile (1930s styling) 1:43	£10-15
☐ US77341	Golden Age Collection set (1940s styling)	£22

98751 Chitty Chitty Bang Bang,
plinth mounted version with certificate.
Sold for £45 DJ Auctions

1176 Scammell Artic truck, Weetabix livery.
An early 1984 post Mattel bankruptcy issue.
Sold for £10 Toy Price Guide Archive

Ref.	Model	Price Guide
❏ US77342	Silver Age Collection set (1950s styling)	£22
❏ US77343	Modern Age Collection 2pce set	£5-10
❏ US77347	Batman Bronze Age Collection 2pce set	£14
❏ US77348	Teen Titan Batmobile	£5-10
❏ US77401	Batcycle	£5-10
❏ US77404	Batcycle	£5-10
❏ US77407	Robin Cycle (mounted figure)	£5-10
❏ US77501	Batmobile (1960s styling)	£5-10
❏ US77505	Batmobile (1960s styling)	£5-10
❏ US77506	Batmobile (1940s styling) 1:24	£15
❏ US77511	Batmobile (2000 styling)	£5-10
❏ US77512	Batmobile (1960s styling), single figure	£5-10
❏ US77601	Batmobile (2004 styling)	£5-10
❏ US77604	Batmobile (2004 styling)	£5-10
❏ US77606	Batmobile Roadster 1:18	£15
❏ US77608	Batmobile Roadster, single figure	£5-10
❏ US77819	Robin Redbird car (2000 styling)	£5-10

Beatles Collection
❏ 4440	Psychedelic Mini (1:36 scale)	£10
❏ 5401	Yellow Submarine (standard size)	£29
❏ 5403	Yellow Sumbarine (1999 issue)	£32
❏ 5404	Yellow Submarine (small)	£7
❏ 5406	Yellow Submarine (with 4 figures)	£19
❏ 5606	Graffiti Bedford Van	£17
❏ 22301	AEC Lorry with advertising board	£19
❏ 32304	Routemaster (1:64 scale), green	£15
❏ 34006	Routemaster, Liverpool Corporation (1:50 scale) yellow version	£18
❏ 35402	Magical Mystery Tour, Bedford Coach	£19
❏ 42403	Magical Mystery Tour, Bedford Coach (1:76 scale)	£21
❏ 58003	Newspaper Taxi, Rita figure	£12
❏ 58007	Newspaper Taxi	£8
❏ BT78211	Yellow submarine	£20
❏ CC05801	Yellow Submarine	£10

Chitty Chitty Bang Bang
❏ 5301	CCBB with Caractacus Potts figure only (plastic wheels)	£21
❏ 5301	CCBB with Caractacus Potts figure only (metal wheels)	£28
❏ 98751	CCBB complete with 4 figures	£25-30
❏ TY87801	CCBB	£12

769 National Express Coach. Early 1984 post Mattel bankruptcy issue.
Sold for £8 Toy Price Guide Archive

CC07802 Transit van, Stan Robinson livery from the Hauliers of Renown series issued in 2006.
Sold for £7 Toy Price Guide Archive

Ref.	Model	Price Guide
Dr Who		
❑ TY96101	Bessie (car) & Dr Who figure	£7
❑ TY96102	Tardis & K9 set	£7
❑ TY96103	Dalek & Cyberman set	£7
❑ TY96104	Dr Who & Davros set	£8-10
❑ TY96201	Bessie (car), Dr Who, Dalek & K9 set	£10-15
❑ TY96202	Cyberman, Davros, Dr Who & Tardis	£10-15
❑ TY96203	40th Anniversary set	£20
Gerry Anderson		
❑ CC00601	Thunderbirds FAB1, matt pink (Collectables Magazine Ltd Ed of 150)	£52
❑ CC00603	Thunderbirds FAB1, pearlescent pink	£10-15
❑ CC00801	Thunderbirds 2 & 4 40th Annivesary set	£10-15
❑ CC96301	Captains Scarlet SPV	£18
❑ CC96302	Captain Scarlet Rhino	£10-15
❑ CC96399	Captain Scarlet SPV & Rhino set	£34
Italian Job		
❑ 4441	Red/white/blue Mini (driver & gold bars)	£15-20
❑ 4443	Mini with gold bars - white (Collect 2000 show)	£25
❑ 5506	3pce Mini set (1:36 scale)	£17
❑ 36502	4pce set (3 x Mini's & Bedford coach)	£208
❑ 97713	3pce Mini set (1:43 scale)	£22
❑ CC82215	Red Mini	£10
❑ CC82217	Mini diorama	£12
❑ CC82249	Mini Team 66 Rally - white	£9
❑ CC86514	Red BMW Mini	£10
❑ CC99138	3pce BMW Mini set	£20
Mr Bean		
❑ 4403	Mini (1:36) 1st issue	£10
❑ 4419	Mini (also 96011)	£10
❑ 4438	Mini with figure	£8
❑ 96011	Mini (1:36), renumbered 04419	£10
❑ CC81201	Mini (1:43)	£10
❑ CC82224	Mini (1:36) with figure	£10
The Muppets		
❑ CC06601	Kermits Car	£5-7
❑ CC06602	Fozzie Bears Car	£5-7
❑ CC06603	Miss Piggy's Car	£5-7
❑ CC06604	Animals Car	£5-7

96682 Inspector Morse Jaguar MkII, maroon with silver trim. Sold for £20 DJ Auctions

24301 Leyland Tanker in Youngers livery from the 1995 Brewery Collection complete with 4 separate documents. Sold for £29 Toy Price Guide Archive

Ref.	Model	Price Guide
Red Dwarf		
❑ CC96501	Stagbug & figure	£8-12
❑ TY96401	Mothership	£8-12
❑ TY96402	Starbug	£8-12
❑ TY96403	Starbug and figures	£10-15
Star Trek (40th Anniversary)		
❑ CC96601	USS Enterprise	£24
❑ CC96602	Bird of Prey	£14
❑ CC96603	USS Enterprise D	£27
❑ CC96607	USS Enterprise	£14
❑ CC96608	Klingon Bird of Prey	£19
OTHER TV FILM		
❑ 101	Avengers Bentley, Steed figure	£17
❑ 502	Z Cars Ford Zephyr	£15
❑ 802	Fawlty Towers Morris 1300, Basil figure	£25
❑ 1801	Buster Jaguar Mk2	£15
❑ 1803	Inspector Morse Jaguar Mk2 - silver trim	£35
❑ 5201	Only Fools & Horses Riliant Regal (1:36)	£10
❑ 7104	Daktari Land Rover, chimp & lion figures	£17
❑ 9002	Dad's Army Thorneycroft Van, Cpl Jones figure	£15
❑ 18302	Moving Story Bedford	£15
❑ 18501	Dad's Army Bedford Van, Hodges figure	£15
❑ 18901	Soldier Soldier Bedford, Robson & Jerome figures	£15
❑ 39901	Elvis Presley Ford Thunderbird, Elvis figure	£18
❑ 39902	Marilyn Monroe Ford Thunderbird, Marilyn figure	£17
❑ 57401	The Professionals Ford Capri	£10-15
❑ 57401	Starsky & Hutch Ford Torino	£10-15
❑ 57403	Kojak's Buick	£24
❑ 54704	Return of the Saint Jaguar XJS, Simon Templar figure	£10-15
❑ 57405	New Avengers Jaguar XJS, Gambit figure	£10-15
❑ 57604	New Avengers Range Rover, Steed figure	£10-15
❑ 96012	Spender Ford Sierra Cosworth	£10-15
❑ 96682	Inspector Morse Jaguar Mk2, no silver silver trim)	£75
❑ 96757	Lovejoy Morris Minor	£10-15
❑ 96758	Some Mothers Do 'Ave 'Em Morris Minor	£10-15
❑ CC00201	Starsky & Hutch Ford Gran Torino	£21
❑ CC00301	Return of the Saint Jaguar XJS	£15-20
❑ CC00401	The Professionals Ford Capri	£15-20
❑ CC00501	Kojak's Buick	£15-20
❑ CC00701	Heartbeat Morris Minor, Oscar Blaketon figure	£10-15

CC10202 Pickfords ERF V Low Loader, issued in 2001. Sold for £22 Toy Price Guide Archive

16703 Pickfords Scammell Highwayman low Loader & Generator load, issued in 1998 with a 4000 Limited Edition. Sold for £41 Toy Price Guide Archive

Ref.	Model	Price Guide
❑ CC01601	Last of the Summer Wine Triumph Herald, single figure	£10-15
❑ CC01701	Heartbeat Morris Minor, Oscar Blaketon figure	£10-15
❑ CC01901	Lock Stock & Two Smoking BarrelsRover 3500, Big Chris figure	£10-15
❑ CC05301	Dukes of Hazzard Dodge Charger, Bo & Luke figures	£10-15
❑ CC05501	Back to the Future De Lorean, Doc figure	£10-15
❑ CC05601	Knight Rider Pontiac Trans Am, Michael Knight figure	£10-15
❑ CC05901	Bullitt Ford Mustang, Steve McQueen figure	£10-15
❑ CC06001	Blues Brothers Dodge Police car, 2 figures	£10-15
❑ CC07002	The Persuaders Aston Martin DB5, Brett Sinclair figure	£10-15
❑ CC07301	Heartbeat Morris truck, Alfred & Greengrass figures	£22
❑ CC07403	Last of the Summer Wine Land Rover, Compo figure	£10-15
❑ CC50902	Green Hornet Black Beauty, Kato figure	£25
❑ CC52405	Monkeemobile	£12
❑ CC54508	Smokey & the Bandit Pontiac TransAm, Bandit figure	£10-15
❑ CC80502	Wallace & Gromit Austin A35 Van, 2 figures	£10-15
❑ CC87501	Charlies Angels Van	£8
❑ CC87502	A Team Van, BA Baracus figure	£10
❑ CC87503	Scooby Doo Mystery Machine Van, Shaggy & Scooby figures	£10
❑ CC99111	Only Fools & Horse Ford Capri & Robin Reliant 2pce set	£15-20

Comic Book Hero Vans (1:43 Scale)

❑ 96846	Tiger Morris 1000	£8-10
❑ 96865	Beezer Ford Popular	£8-10
❑ 96887	Topper Morris J	£8-10
❑ 96961	Lion VW	£8-10
❑ 98754	Adventure Bedford Van	£8-10
❑ 98755	The Hotspur Ford Popular	£8-10
❑ 98756	The Rover Morris 1000	£8-10
❑ 98757	Skipper VW	£8-10
❑ 98758	Wizard Morris J	£8-10
❑ 98759	Dandy Morris J & Bedford 2pce set	£10-15
❑ 98960	Beano Morris 2pce set	£10-15
❑ 98965	Eagle Bedford & VW 2pce set	£10-15
❑ 98970	X-Men Bedford & morris 2pce set	£10-15
❑ 98972	Spiderman Morris 2pce set	£10-15
❑ 98973	Captain America Ford Popular & VW set	£10-15
❑ D14/1	Beano & Dandy Bedford Van 2pce set	£20-25
❑ D47/1	Beano AEC bus & Morris J 2pce set	£10-15

Royal Coach Issues

❑ 37003	State Landau - Queen Mother's 100th Birthday model, 2 figures	£19
❑ CC09901	State Landau - Queen Elizabeth II Golden Jubilee	£34

A pair of Cameo Collection models from
1992 made in Great Britain.
Sold for 50p each Toy Price Guide Archive

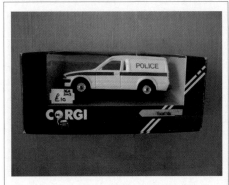

621 Police Escort van, 1984 issue in early blue box.
Sold for £9 Toy Price Guide Archive

Ref.	Model	Range	Price Guide

AMERICAN SERIES

Yellow Coach 743

❑ 53901	Union Pacific	£15
❑ 53903	Eastern Michigan	£15-20
❑ 53905	Washington Motor Coach	£15-20
❑ 53906	Greyhound - Kansas destination	£15-20
❑ 53907	Baltimore & Ohio	£15-20
❑ 98462	Greyhound - Chicago destination	£13
❑ 98462	Greyhound - Atlanta destination	£15
❑ 98460	Greyhound - NY World Fair	£13
❑ 98461	Greyhound - Philadelphia destination	£14
❑ 98464	Burlingham	£17
❑ 98465	Burlingham	£16
❑ 98467	New Jersey	£15-20
❑ 98468	Champlain	£15-20
❑ 98469	Greyhound - LA destination	£15-20
❑ 98470	Silverside	£15-20
❑ 98472	The WAC Needs You	£15-20
❑ 98473	Join the Waves	£15-20
❑ 98741	Greyhound - San Fransisco destination	£15-20
❑ US53908	Gray Coach Lines - Canada	£15-20
❑ US53909	Greyhound - Pittsburgh destination	£15-20

GM Bus

❑ 54001	Surface Transportation	£14-18
❑ 54002	Madison Avenue	£14-18
❑ 54003	St. Louis	£14-18
❑ 54004	New York	£14-18
❑ 54005	Public Service	£14-18
❑ 54006	Wabash Railway	£14-18
❑ 54008	Market St. Railway	£14-18
❑ 54009	New England Transportation	£14-18
❑ 54010	Chicago	£14-18
❑ 54012	Greyhound	£14-18
❑ 54014	Fruit Salad	£14-18
❑ 54015	Texaco	£14-18
❑ 54101	Greyhound	£14-18
❑ 54102	Red Arrow	£14-18
❑ 54104	Peerless Stages	£14-18
❑ 54106	New Haven	£14-18
❑ 54201	Worcester Bus Co	£14-18

1993 issue Police Escort van in later window packaging. Sold for £6 Toy Price Guide Archive

40101 OOC Weymann Trolleybus, Maidstone Corporation livery issued in 1995. Sold for £14 Toy Price Guide Archive

Ref.	Model	Range	Price Guide
❏ 54202	Greyhound		£14-18
❏ 54203	New Jersey		£14-18
❏ 97635	Los Angeles		£14-18
❏ 98600	Pacific Greyhound		£14-18
❏ 98601	Pacific Electric		£14-18
❏ 98602	Greyhound		£14-18
❏ 98603	Detroit		£14-18
❏ 98604	5th Avenue		£14-18
❏ US54017	De Camp		£14-18
❏ US54018	Corgi City		£14-18
❏ US54019	Green Bus lines		£14-18
❏ US54021	Carolina Trailways		£22
GM5300 Bus			
❏ 54301	New York		£25-30
❏ 54303	Trailways (Ltd Ed 5000)		£53
❏ 54304	Los Angeles		£25-30
❏ 54305	Toronto		£25-30
❏ 54306	Golden Gate		£25-30
❏ 54307	Greyhound - NY World Fair		£25-30
❏ 54402	Greyhound		£25-30
❏ 54501	San Diego		£25-30
❏ 54502	Pennsylvannia		£25-30
❏ 54503	Greyhound - NY World Fair		£25-30
❏ 54504	Santa Monica		£25-30
❏ 54507	Liberty Lines		£25-30
❏ 54601	DC Transit		£25-30
❏ 54602	Chicago		£25-30
❏ 54603	AC Transit		£25-30
❏ 54604	Philadelphia		£25-30
❏ 54605	Reading		£25-30
❏ US54308	NY Transit		£25-30
❏ US54309	Gray Coach Lines		£25-30
❏ US54310	Chicago		£25-30
❏ US54311	Baltimore		£25-30
❏ US54312	NY Metropolitan		£25-30
❏ US54313	NY Bus Lines		£25-30
❏ US54316	Fishbowl - NY World Fair		£25-30
❏ US54317	Command Bus Line - NY		£25-30
MC1 102 DL3 Bus			
❏ 53401	Greyhound		£25-30

97814 AEC Regent II London Passenger Transport
Board, 11000 Limited Edition issued in 1995.
Sold for £14 Toy Price Guide Archive

97944 Leyland PD2 Newcastle Corporation,
15000 Limited Edition issued in 1995.
Sold for £12 Toy Price Guide Archive

Ref.	Model	Range	Price Guide
❏ 98421	Demonstration bus		£25-30
❏ 98422	Peter Pan Trailways		£25-30
❏ 98427	Peter Pan birthday bus		£25-30
❏ 98652	PCST Sea World		£25-30
❏ US53403	Coach USA		£25-30
❏ US53404	Greyhound - 6018		£25-30
❏ US53405	Greyhound - TNM&O		£25-30
❏ US53407	Bonanza		£25-30
❏ US53409	Gray Coach Lines - NY		£25-30

PCC Street Car

❏ 55001	Philadelphia		£28-35
❏ 55002	San Francisco		£28-35
❏ 55003	St Louis		£28-35
❏ 55005	Cincinnati		£28-35
❏ 55006	Pacific Electric		£28-35
❏ 55007	Los Angeles		£28-35
❏ 55008	Boston		£28-35
❏ 55009	Washington		£28-35
❏ 55010	Toronto		£28-35
❏ 55010	20th Anniversary BRITACAN model		£28-35
❏ 55013	Pittsburgh		£28-35
❏ 55014	Minneapolis		£28-35
❏ 55016	New Jersey		£28-35
❏ 55017	Johnstown		£28-35
❏ US55018	Pittsburgh - route 23		£28-35
❏ US55019	Capital Transit		£28-35
❏ US55020	New Jersey		£28-35
❏ US55021	Los Angeles - Fruit Salad		£28-35
❏ US55022	Budweiser		£28-35
❏ US55023	Brooklyn		£28-35
❏ US55024	Baltimore		£28-35
❏ US55026	Detroit		£28-35
❏ US55027	Chicago		£28-35
❏ US55028	Kenosha		£28-35
❏ US55029	Boston Centenary model		£28-35
❏ US55030	Pittsburgh - Port Authority		£28-35
❏ US55031	SE Pennsylvannia		£28-35

GM4501 Scenicruiser

❏ US54405	Greyhound - Pittsburgh		£25-30
❏ US54406	Greyhound - Chicago		£28-35

05603 Bedford CA KLG Plugs van, 5000 Limited Edition from the Corgi Archive collection issued in 1997. Sold for £6 Toy Price Guide Archive

Code 2 for the North East Diecast Collectors Club produced in 2000. Sold for £19 Toy Price Guide Archive

Ref.	Model	Range	Price Guide
US54409	Washington DC		£28-35
US54410	Boston		£28-35
US54415	Greyhound - Sann Francisco		£28-35
US54417	Greyhound - bare casting		£28-35
US54418	Greyhound - St Louis		£28-35
Birney Safety Car (1:48)			
US55202	Steinway - NY		£28-35
US55203	Philadelphia		£28-35
US55204	Baltimore (Ltd Ed 1980)		£37
US55205	Fort Collins		£28-35
US55206	Chicago		£28-35
Flexible Clipper			
US54204	Greyhound - Cleveland		NPA
US54205	Capital Bus Co		£37
TRUCKS & COMMERCIALS			
50102	M151 Mutt Utility - Texaco		£20-25
50201	M35 Deuce - Texaco		£20-25
50601	Mack - MKT		£8
50701	Mack - Merchants		£20-25
50702	Mack - Schaefer Beer		£20-25
50703	Mack - Guinness		£20-25
50704	Mack - Mason Dixon		£20-25
50901	Mack - Mobilgas		£20-25
51001	Mack - Richfield		£20-25
51002	Mack - Flying Gasoline		£20-25
52301	Mack - Great Northern Railway		£11
52303	Mack - Nickel Plate Road		£20-25
52304	Mack - Ballantines Beer		£20-25
52306	Mack - Carolina		£20-25
52501	Mack - NY Central		£14
52504	Mack - Milwaukee Road		£12
52801	Mack - Railway Express		£11
52802	Mack - Burlington		£20-25
52901	Diamond T620 - Iron City Beer		£15-20
52902	Diamond T620, drum load - Texaco		£15-20
52903	Diamond T620, crate load - Guinness		£20-25
53101	Diamond T620 - Greyhound Van Lines		£20-25
53201	Mack - Shell		£20-25
53202	Mack - Sinclair		£20-25

Ref.	Model	Range	Price Guide
❏ 53203	Mack - Union 76		£20-25
❏ 53301	Mack - White Rose		£20-25
❏ 53302	Mack - Texaco		£20-25
❏ 53502	Mack - Campbell Express		£20-25
❏ 53503	Mack with Luffing Shovel - Texaco		£20-25
❏ 53601	Mack wrecker - AND		£15-20
❏ 53603	Mack wrecker - CAA		£15-20
❏ 55301	Diamond T980, generator load - Allied (Ltd Ed 5000)		£52
❏ 55304	Diamond T980 - Texaco		£50-60
❏ 55606	Diamond T wrecker - Public Service Inc		£50-60
❏ 55610	Diamond T wrecker - Texaco		£50-60
❏ 55801	Kenworth W925 - Guinness		£25-35
❏ 55802	Kenworth W925 - Navajo		£25-35
❏ 55901	Diamond T620 - Motor Car Co (Ltd Ed 5000)		£25-35
❏ 56201	Diamond T620 tanker - Gulf		£25-35
❏ 56202	Diamons T tanker - Cities Service		£25-35
❏ 56203	Diamond T tanker - Superfest		£25-35
❏ 56204	Diamond T620 tanker - Texaco		£25-35
❏ 56301	Diamond T620 - Richfield		£25-35
❏ 56401	Diamond T620 - Schlitz Beer		£15-20
❏ 56404	Diamond T620 - Guinness		£25-35
❏ 97469	Ford Model T - Victorola		£7
❏ 98481	Mack - Good Year		£11
❏ 98449	White tanker - Petrol Co		£10
❏ 98458	White - Jacob Rupperts		£10-15
❏ 98459	White - XXX		£10-15
❏ 98457	White - White Rock		£10-15
❏ 98456	White - Scheiwes Coal		£10-15
❏ 98455	White - Pennsylvannia Stores		£10-15
❏ 98453	Mack - Breyer		£10-15
❏ 98454	Mack - Wilton Dairy		£10-15
❏ US51405	Mack - Vernors Ginger Ale		£10-15
❏ US51405	International Transtar		£10-15
❏ US52308	Mack wrecker - Texaco		£10-15
❏ US52309	Mack - Moosehead		£10-15
❏ US52310	Mack - Budweiser		£10-15
❏ US52905	Diamond T620 - Moosehead		£10-15
❏ US52912	Diamond T620 - Chicago		£10-15
❏ US52913	Diamond T620 - 7UP		£10-15
❏ US55703	Kenworth W925 tanker - Texaco		£35-40
❏ US55709	Kenworth with boat load (Ltd Ed 1680)		£35-40

Ref.	Model	Range	Price Guide
Heavy Haulage			
❏ US50705	Mack - Litefoot Logging (Ltd Ed 4000)		£40-50
❏ US50706	Mack - Budweiser sign load		£40-50
❏ US50710	Mack, hay load		£57
❏ US51401	International Transtar, girder load		£40-50
❏ US51402	International Transtar - Texas Pipeline		£50-60
❏ US51403	International Transtar - Sulley Trucking		£40-50
❏ US51404	International Transtar - Lindquist Trucking		£40-50
❏ US55103	Diamond T989 - Gerosa		£29
❏ US55109	Diamond T989, house load		£25-30
❏ US55702	Kenworth W925, boiler load		£42
❏ US55704	Kenworth W925 - Texas Pipeline		£49
❏ US55705	Kenworth W925 - Interstate Heavy Hauling		£40-50
❏ US55706	Kenworth W925, culvert load - Cast Transport		£40-50
❏ US55708	Kenworth W925 with Lowboy trailer		£40-50
FIRE			
❏ US52605	Ahrens Fox Piston Pumper - Washington		£20
American La France Aerial Rescue			
❏ 51802	Rochester, NY		£20-25
❏ 51901	Boston		£20-25
❏ 97320	Re-issue of early Corgi 1143 model		£19
❏ 97321	Centreville		£20-25
❏ 97324	Orlando		£20-25
❏ 97387	Denver		£20-25
❏ 97398	Jersey City		£20-25
American La France Pumper			
❏ 51501	Westminster		£15-20
❏ 51502	Bethpage		£15-20
❏ 51701	Staten Island		£15-20
❏ 51702	Baltimore		£15-20
❏ 97322	Chicago		£15-20
❏ 97323	Carnegie		£15-20
❏ 97325	Denver		£15-20
❏ 97326	Orlando		£15-20
❏ 97387	Wayne		£15-20
❏ 97395	Vero Beach		£15-20
❏ US51503	San Francisco		£15-20

Ref.	Model	Range	Price Guide
American La France 700 Pumper			
☐ US53504	Elkhart		£15-20
☐ US53505	Baltimore Co		£15-20
☐ US53506	Washington DC		£15-20
☐ CC53507	Washington Fire Co		£15-20
☐ US53508	Boston - open cab		£15-20
☐ US53509	Boston - closed cab		£15-20
☐ US53510	Denver		£15-20
☐ US53513	Bethpage		£15-20
☐ US54509	Brook Park		£15-20
E One Cyclone Rescue			
☐ 52201	Rescue		£20-25
☐ 52202	Schaumburg		£20-25
☐ 52203	Long Lake		£20-25
☐ 52204	Washington DC		£20-25
☐ 52205	Boston		£20-25
☐ 52206	Baltimore		£20-25
E One 75ft Ladder			
☐ 54901	Demonstrator		£20-25
☐ 54902	Duncan		£20-25
☐ 54903	Bartlett		£20-25
☐ 54904	Titusville		£20-25
☐ US54905	Anne Arundel		£20-25
E One Pumper			
☐ 54701	Boston		£20-25
☐ 54702	Fort Monroe		£20-25
☐ 54703	Newark		£20-25
☐ 54704	Shippenburg		£20-25
☐ 54705	East Hazel		£20-25
☐ 54706	Washington DC		£20-25
☐ 54801	Fishers		£20-25
☐ 54802	Seattle		£20-25
☐ US52207	Kansas city		£20-25
☐ US52208	Fairfax County		£20-25
☐ US52209	Washington DC		£20-25
☐ 54506	GM 5300 mobile Command Center - Peoria		£20-25
☐ US50207	M35 Brush Truck - New Jersey		£20-25

Ref.	Model	Range	Price Guide
Mack B Aerial Ladder			
❑ 52701	Chicago		£20-25
❑ 52702	Wilkes - Barre		£20-25
Mack B Pumper			
❑ 52401	Elkridge		£15-20
❑ 52403	Corpus Christi		£15-20
❑ 52404	Baltic		£15-20
❑ 52601	Malvern		£15-20
❑ 52602	Gettysburg		£15-20
❑ 52603	Lampeter		£15-20
❑ 98486	Paxtonia		£15-20
❑ 98450	Chicago		£15-20
❑ US52307	Texaco		£15-20
❑ 53602	Mack B Wrecker - Chicago		£15-20
Mack CF Aerial Ladder			
❑ 52101	Long Beach		£25-30
❑ 52102	Milwaukee		£25-30
❑ 52103	Allentown		£25-30
Mack CF Tower Ladder			
❑ 53801	Allentown		£25-30
❑ US53803	San Francisco		£25-30
❑ US53804	Philadelphia		£25-30
❑ US53805	Bethpage		£25-30
❑ US53806	Green Tree		£25-30
❑ US53807	Mahonoy City		£25-30
❑ US53205	Mack C Pumper - Baltimore		£15-20
Mack CF Pumper			
❑ 52001	Jersey City		£15-20
❑ 52003	Napa City		£15-20
❑ 52004	St Mary's County		£15-20
❑ 52005	Lodi		£15-20
❑ 98484	Chicago		£15-20
❑ 98485	Neptune		£15-20
❑ 98451	Berwick		£15-20
❑ US52007	Engine Co		£15-20
❑ US52008	Bethpage		£15-20

Ref.	Model	Range	Price Guide
❏ US52009	Tamaqua		£15-20
❏ US52804	Mack L Pumper - Chicago		£15-20
❏ US53003	Maxim Pumper - Valhalla		£15-20
❏ US53103	REO Speedwagon - Shippenburg		£25-30

Seagrave Anniversary Pumper
Ref.	Model	Range	Price Guide
❏ US50501	Columbus		£25-30
❏ US50502	Tampa		£25-30
❏ US50503	Miami		£25-30
❏ US50506	New Have		£25-30
❏ US50508	Vigilant Hose Co		£25-30
❏ US50511	Kensington		£25-30
❏ US50512	Kentland		£25-30
❏ US50509	Seagrave Sedan (70th Anniversary) - Tenafly		£30-35

Seagrave Aerial (70th Anniversary)
Ref.	Model	Range	Price Guide
❏ US52506	Baltimore		£30-35
❏ US52507	Boston		£30-35
❏ US52508	Shippenburg		£30-35
❏ US52511	Columbus		£30-35

Seagrave K
Ref.	Model	Range	Price Guide
❏ US50801	Jackson		£30-35
❏ US50802	NASA		£30-35
❏ US50803	Engine Co		£30-35
❏ US50804	Baltimore		£30-35
❏ US50805	Baltimore County		£30-35
❏ US50806	Fairfax County		£30-35
❏ US50807	Kansas City		£30-35
❏ US50808	Washington		£30-35
❏ US50809	Los Angeles		£30-35
❏ US50810	Harrison, NY		£30-35
❏ US50504	Seagrave Safety Sedan Pumper - Detroit		£30-35
❏ 98452	White Tanker - Volunteer Fire Dept		£15-20

Ref.	Model	Range	Price Guide
Chevrolet			
❏ 51201	Centrville		£8-13
❏ 51301	San Diego		£8-13
❏ 51303	NYPD		£8-13
❏ 51304	Nassau Police		£8-13
❏ 51306	Ontario Police		£8-13
❏ 97389	Chicago Fire Chief's car		£8-13
❏ 97396	Highway Patrol		£8-13
❏ 97397	Pensacola Fire Chief's car		£8-13
Dodge Monaco			
❏ US50602	Battalion Chief's car		£8-13
❏ US06004	Chicago Police		£8-13
❏ US06005	California Highway Patrol		£8-13
❏ US06006	NY State Police		£8-13
Helicopter			
❏ US33409	Sikorsky - LA Sheriff's Dept		£25-30
❏ US50401	Huey - LA Fire Dept		£25-30
❏ US51903	H47 - Chicago Police Dept		£25-30
❏ US51905	Bell 47 - NYPD		£25-30
Sets			
❏ US99150	Detroit 2pce Commemorative set		£127
US MILITARY			
❏ US34206	Chinook Helicopter - Guns a Go Go		£15-20
❏ US35902	Blackhawk Helicopter - Southern Iraq		£15-20
❏ US50308	M48 A3 - 11th Cavalry		£15-20
❏ US50309	1st Tank Sqadron - Disaster		£15-20
❏ US50411	Huey Helicopter - 174th Assault		£15-20
❏ US50412	Huey Helicopter - Marine Corp		£15-20
❏ US51104	M113 ACAV - Draft Dodger		£15-20
❏ US51105	M113 ACAV - 8th Infantry		£15-20
❏ US51207	Cobra - Development Squadron		£15-20
❏ US51208	Cobra - Widow Maker		£15-20
❏ 50101	Mutt Utility Truck	Unsung Heroes	£20-25
❏ 50202	Duece & 2.5 Ton Truck	Unsung Heroes	£20-25
❏ 50301	A3 Main Battle Tank - Patton	Unsung Heroes	£20-25
❏ 50401	Gunship Helicopter - Huey Hog	Unsung Heroes	£20-25
❏ US50103	Mutt Recoiless Gun & Trailer	Unsung Heroes	£20-25
❏ US50105	Mutt Utility Truck - USAF	Unsung Heroes	£20-25

Ref.	Model	Range	Price Guide
❑ US50204	2.5 Ton Truck - USAF	Unsung Heroes	£20-25
❑ US50206	Gun Truck - Gamblers	Unsung Heroes	£20-25
❑ US50303	M48 Patton Tank - US Army	Unsung Heroes	£20-25
❑ US50306	A3 Tank - C Company, 3rd Marine Division	Unsung Heroes	£20-25
❑ US50307	M48 Tank - TULA	Unsung Heroes	£20-25
❑ US50402	UH-IC Huey Frog Helicopter	Unsung Heroes	£20-25
❑ US50403	UH-IC Huey Frog Gunship Helicopter	Unsung Heroes	£20-25
❑ US50405	UH-IC Huey Helicopter - US Army Medevac	Unsung Heroes	£20-25
❑ US50409	Bell Huey Gunship Helicopter	Unsung Heroes	£20-25
❑ US50410	UH-IC Helicopter - 1st Cavalry	Unsung Heroes	£20-25
❑ US51101	M113 Armoured Cavalry Assault Vehicle - US Army	Unsung Heroes	£20-25
❑ US51102	M106 Mortar Truck - US Army	Unsung Heroes	£20-25
❑ US51103	M113 Ambulance - 9th Infantry	Unsung Heroes	£20-25
❑ US51202	Bell AH-IC Huey Cobra Helecopter - USMC	Unsung Heroes	£20-25
❑ US51204	Cobra Helecopter - HML 367	Unsung Heroes	£20-25
❑ US51205	AH-1G Helecopter - 1st Cavalry, The Crystal	Unsung Heroes	£20-25

Korean War Vehicles

Ref.	Model	Range	Price Guide
❑ US33013	Corsair - USS Badoeng Strait	Forgotten Heroes	£20-25
❑ US51003	Sherman Flame Tank - USMC	Forgotten Heroes	£20-25
❑ US51008	Sherman Tank - Tiger Face	Forgotten Heroes	£20-25
❑ US51027	Sherman Tank - US Army	Forgotten Heroes	£20-25
❑ US51601	T34/85 Tank - North Korean 109th Regiment	Forgotten Heroes	£20-25
❑ US51604	T34/85 Tank - Naktong River, Korea	Forgotten Heroes	£20-25
❑ US51703	WC51 Weapons Carrier - US Army	Forgotten Heroes	£20-25
❑ US51902	Bell Helicopter - US Medical Corps	Forgotten Heroes	£20-25
❑ US51904	Bell H13 HMX-1 Helicopter	Forgotten Heroes	£20-25
❑ US51906	Bell Helicopter - Korea 1951	Forgotten Heroes	£20-25
❑ US60415	Machine Gun Motor Carriage - Korea 1951	Forgotten Heroes	£20-25
❑ US51026	Sherman Tank	World War II	NPA
❑ US60511	Tiger Tank	World War II	NPA
❑ US61001	D-Day Surrender - diorama set 1	World War II	£61
❑ US61002	D-Day Surrender - diorama set 2	World War II	£67
❑ US61003	Arnhem Bridge - diorama set 1	World War II	£59
❑ US61004	Arnhem Bridge - diorama set 2	World War II	£62

1:64 Scale

Ref.	Model	Range	Price Guide
❑ US95102	US Army Infantry Set	Tactical Strike	NPA
❑ US95103	USMC Infantry Set	Tactical Strike	NPA
❑ US95104	Avenger Missile System - US Army	Tactical Strike	NPA
❑ US95105	Avenger Missile System - USMC	Tactical Strike	NPA
❑ US95112	Bradley Fighting Vehicle - US Army	Tactical Strike	NPA

Trio of US, British & French military
Diamond T Wrecker Tank Transporters.
Sold for £95 DJ Auctions

Pair of Diamond T Wreckers comprising Generator
load & similar French Bourgey Montreuil issue.
Sold for £60 DJ Auctions

Ref.	Model	Range	Price Guide
❏ US95121	AH-6J Helicopter - Little Bird	Tactical Strike	NPA
❏ US95122	Abrams Tank - US Army	Tactical Strike	NPA
❏ US95123	Abrams Tank - USMC	Tactical Strike	NPA
❏ US95132	Apache Helicopter - US Army	Tactical Strike	NPA
❏ US95141	Tomcat - Bounty Hunters	Tactical Strike	NPA

LIONEL CITY/LIONELVILLE

Ref.	Model	Range	Price Guide
❏ 51302	Cheverolet Sheriff car	Lionel City	£17-22
❏ 51801	American La France Aerial Ladder	Lionel City	£18
❏ 52002	Mack CF Pumper	Lionel City	£17-22
❏ 52302	Mack B Semi Trailer	Lionel City	£17-22
❏ 52402	Mack B Pumper	Lionel City	£17-22
❏ 52503	Mack B van	Lionel City	£17-22
❏ 53501	Mack B Semi Dropside	Lionel City	£17-22
❏ 53902	Yellow Coach - Lionel Bus Lines	Lionel City	£17-22
❏ 53904	Yellow Coach - Lionel City Bus Lines	Lionel City	£17-22
❏ 54007	GM4502 Coach	Lionel City	£17-22
❏ 54011	GM4507 Coach	Lionel City	£17-22
❏ 54103	GM4507 Coach	Lionel City	£17-22
❏ 54302	GM5301 Coach - Lionel City Transit	Lionel City	£17-22
❏ 54401	GM5301 Coach - Lionel City Bus Services	Lionel City	£17-22
❏ 54404	GM5301 Coach	Lionel City	£17-22
❏ 55004	PCC Street Car	Lionel City	£17-22
❏ US06007	Dodge Monaco - Police Dept	Lionelville	£27
❏ US50602	Mack AC Truck - Hood & Sons	Lionelville	£27
❏ US50708	Mack LJ Flatbed - NY Central Railroad	Lionelville	£24
❏ US52315	Mack B Wrecker	Lionelville	£29
❏ US52906	Diamond T620 - Lion Oil	Lionelville	£19
❏ US52908	Diamond T620 - Pennsylvania Railroad	Lionelville	£25-30
❏ US52311	Mack B Lowboy with Luffing Shovel	Lionelville	£25-30
❏ US54412	Greyhound Scenic Cruiser - Lionelville	Lionelville	£25-30
❏ US74503	White Flatbed - Pine Peak Christmas Tree Farms	Lionelville	£25-30

SETS

Ref.	Model	Range	Price Guide
❏ 97049	Yellowstone Park 2pce set		£11

Pickfords and another Diamond T Wreckers with
load. Sold for £50 DJ Auctions

French Heritage Avec Rouleau STAG with
Diamond T. Sold for £70 DJ Auctions

Ref.	Model	Price Guide

COLLECTION HERITAGE - FRANCE

Ref.	Model	Price Guide
55303	Diamond T980, transformer load - Bourgey	£50
55607	Diamond T Wrecker - Renault Service	£30-35
70001	Berliet Tanker - Chambourcy (Ltd Ed 4000)	£38
70402	Berliet Wrecker	£30-35
70503	Renault 1000KG - Renault Service	£15-20
70504	Renault 1000KG - Shell	£15-20
70506	Renault 1000KG & trailer - Renault Cinema	£15-20
70507	Renault 1000KG - Mazda	£15-20
70508	Renault 1000KG - Evian	£15-20
70510	Renault 1000KG - Berger	£15-20
70603	Peugeot D3A - Peugeot Service	£15-20
70606	Peugeot D3A - Cibie	£15-20
70607	Peugeot D3A - Milko	£15-20
70608	Peugeot D3A - Nestle	£15-20
71001	Renault dropside - Michelin	£15-20
71004	Renault dropside - Renault	£15-20
71006	Renault	£15-20
71101	Renault dropside with barrels - Limonades Dumesnil	£15-20
71102	Renault dropside - Hules Renault	£15-20
71104	Renault dropside - Orangina	£15-20
71105	Renault dropside - Vichy Etat	£15-20
71106	Saviem dropside - Perrier	£15-20
71201	Renault Tanker - Total	£15-20
71204	Renault Tanker - Esso	£15-20
71206	Renault Tanker - Shell	£15-20
71207	Faineant tanker - Antar	£15-20
71301	Renault van - Perrier	£15-20
71401	Renault van - Valentine (Ltd Ed 4000)	£26
71403	Renault van - Calberson	£15-20
71405	Renault van - SiC	£15-20
71406	Renault van - Pschitt	£15-20
71407	Renault van - Renault Services	£15-20
71408	Saviem van - Cirage Cream	£15-20
71409	Saviem van - Nescafe	£15-20
71411	Faineant van - Bazar, Hotel de Ville	£15-20
71412	Faineant van - Banania	£15-20
71501	Saviem JL box van - Michelin	£25-30
71502	Saviem JL box van - Suchard	£25-30
71505	Saviem JL box van - Laiteterie Parisienne	£25-30
71601	Saviem dropside - Renault Agricole	£25-30

Wynns Heavy Haulage Diamond T Ballast
24 Wheel Girder Trailer with Boiler Load.
Sold for £45 DJ Auctions

A trio of Bus sets including east Kent, York Brothers
& Yelloway. Sold for £32 DJ Auctions

Ref.	Model	Price Guide
❏ 71701	Saviem & trailer - Calberson	£25-30
❏ 71801	Saviem JL tanker - BP	£25-30
❏ 71802	Renault JL20 tanker - Pere Bonoit	£25-30
❏ 71902	Saviem JL van - Consortium Rondeau	£25-30
❏ 72001	Bernard van - Danone	£25-30
❏ 72002	Bernard van - Calberson Flageul	£25-30
❏ 72003	Bernard van - Lustucru (Ltd Ed 4000)	£37
❏ 72005	Bernard van - Saint Marc (Ltd Ed 3500)	£27
❏ 72006	Bernard van - Menier	£25-30
❏ 72007	Bernard van - Ricques	£25-30
❏ 72008	Bernard van - Aiguebelles	£25-30
❏ 72009	Bernard van - Gondolo	£25-30
❏ 72010	Bernard van - Courvoisier	£25-30
❏ 72011	Bernard van - Berger	£25-30
❏ 72101	Bernard tanker - Saint Gobain	£25-30
❏ 72801	Unic Saverne - Calberson	£13-17
❏ 72803	Unic Saverne - Phillips	£13-17
❏ 72805	Unic Saverne - BIC	£13-17
❏ 72901	Saviem flatbed - Simca	£13-17
❏ 72902	Simca dropside - Ripolin	£13-17
❏ 72903	Simca dropside - Villeroy & Boch	£13-17
❏ 72904	Simca tanker - Azur	£13-17
❏ 72907	Simca tanker - Purfina	£13-17
❏ 72908	Simca van - Bailly	£15-20
❏ 72910	Simca glass truck - Saint Gobain	£13-17
❏ 72911	Simca cargo truck - L'Air Liquide	£13-17
❏ 72913	Simca tanker - BP	£13-17
❏ 73001	Berliet van - L'Alsacienne (Ltd Ed 4000)	£31
❏ 73002	Berliet van - Banania	£25-30
❏ 73003	Berliet van - Gringoire (Ltd Ed 5000)	£32
❏ 73004	Berliet van - Orangina	£30-35
❏ 73005	Berliet van - Roquefort	£30-35
❏ 73006	Berliet van - Vitapointe	£30-35
❏ 73007	Berliet van - Berger	£30-35
❏ 73101	Berliet flatbed - Vini Prix (Ltd Ed 4000)	£32
❏ 73201	Berliet tanker - Shell	£30-35
❏ 73601	Berliet dropside - Le Fevre Utile	£30-35
❏ 73602	Berliet articulated trailer - Amora	£30-35
❏ 73701	Berliet articulated trailer - Shell	£30-35
❏ 74002	Citroen Type 55 tilt - lefranc	£30-35
❏ 74101	Citroen Type 55 van - La Vache Serieuse	£30-35
❏ 74102	Citroen Type 55 van - Michelin	£30-35

Ref.	Model	Price Guide
❏ 74103	Citroen Type 55 van - Chambourcy	£30-35
❏ 74201	Citroen Type 55 low loader - Bourgey Monteuil	£30-35
❏ 74202	Citroen Type 55 low loader - Calberson	£30-35
❏ 74601	Citroen Type 55 tanker - Dynavia	£30-35
❏ 74602	Citroen Type 55 tanker - Shell	£30-35
❏ 74701	Citroen Type 55 dropside - Gini	£30-35
❏ 74702	Citroen Type 55 dropside - Berger	£30-35
❏ 74801	Citroen Type 55 van - Citroen	£30-35
❏ EX55105	Diamond T980 - STAG	£30-35
❏ EX70202	Berliet van - Michelin	£30-35
❏ EX70203	Berliet flatbed, barrel load - Henri Walbaum	£30-35
❏ EX70204	Berliet van - Berger	£30-35
❏ EX70205	Berliet van - Portenseigne	£30-35
❏ EX70206	Berliet artic - STAG	£30-35
❏ EX70207	Berliet & trailer - Postes	£30-35
❏ EX70511	Renault 1000KG van - Chambourcy	£13-17
❏ EX70512	Renault 1000KG van - Michelin	£13-17
❏ EX70513	Renault 1000KG van - Lampes Claude	£13-17
❏ EX70514	Renault 1000KG van - Renault	£13-17
❏ EX70515	Renault 1000KG van - Valentine	£13-17
❏ EX70516	Renault 1000KG van - Baroclem	£13-17
❏ EX70517	Renault 1000KG van - Schneider	£13-17
❏ EX70518	Renault 1000KG van - RITA	£13-17
❏ EX70524	Renault 1000KG van - Ricard	£13-17
❏ EX70525	Renault 1000KG van - Gondolo	£13-17
❏ EX70527	Renault 1000KG van - Aspro	£13-17
❏ EX70529	Renault 1000KG van - Nescafe	£13-17
❏ EX70530	Renault 1000KG van - Ricqles	£13-17
❏ EX70531	Renault 1000KG van - Rondeau	£13-17
❏ EX70532	Renault 1000KG van - Berger	£13-17
❏ EX70533	Renault 1000KG van - Royal Mint Gum	£13-17
❏ EX70535	Renault 1000KG van - Chicoree Williot	£13-17
❏ EX70537	Renault 1000KG van - Milliat Freres	£13-17
❏ EX70539	Renault 1000KG van, bottles on roof	£13-17
❏ EX70540	Renault 1000KG van, loudspeaker on roof - Pernod	£13-17
❏ EX70610	Peugeot D3A van - Postes	£13-17
❏ EX70611	Peugeot D3A van - Oringina	£13-17
❏ EX70612	Peugeot D3A van - Brandt	£13-17
❏ EX70613	Peugeot D3A van - St Breiuc	£13-17
❏ EX70614	Peugeot D3A van - Chenard & Walker	£13-17
❏ EX70615	Peugeot D3A van - Michelin	£13-17
❏ EX70616	Peugeot D3A van - Montel de Gelat	£13-17

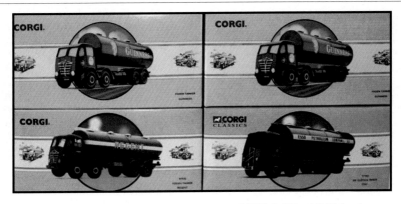

4 Corgi classic Foden Tankers; 2 Guinness, Regent & ESSO. Sold for £65 DJ Auctions

Ref.	Model	Price Guide
❑ EX70620	Peugeot D3A van - Post van	£13-17
❑ EX70621	Peugeot D3A van - Peugeot	£13-17
❑ EX70622	Peugeot D3A minibus, blue	£13-17
❑ EX70623	Peugeot D3A minibus, red/white	£13-17
❑ EX70624	Peugeot D3A van - Atlantic	£13-17
❑ EX70625	Peugeot D3A van - Pernod	£13-17
❑ EX70628	Peugeot D3A van - Lait Mont Blanc	£13-17
❑ EX70629	Peugeot D3A van - Faraghi	£13-17
❑ EX70630	Peugeot D3A van - Lyons Motorcycles	£13-17
❑ EX70631	Peugeot D3A van - Michelin	£13-17
❑ EX70632	Peugeot D3A van - BP Peugeot	£13-17
❑ EX70633	Peugeot D3A van - Chicoree Williot	£13-17
❑ EX70724	Peugeot D3A van - Atlantic	£13-17
❑ EX70902	Renault JL20 with trailer - Michelin	£20-25
❑ EX70904	Renault JL20 artic - Dunlop	£20-25
❑ EX70906	Renault JL20 artic - Saint Gobain	£20-25
❑ EX70911	Saviem Citerne - Total	£20-25
❑ EX71007	Renault van - Transports de L'Orme	£20-25
❑ EX71008	Faineant van - Pere la Grolle	£20-25
❑ EX72012	Bernard van - Delices	£20-25
❑ EX72014	Bernard 9A90 - St Raphael Quinquina	£20-25
❑ EX72914	Simca cargo truck - SNCF	£20-25
❑ EX74003	Citroen Type 55 - Bache	£20-25
❑ EX74005	Citroen Type 55 dropside - L'Air Liquide	£20-25
EMERGENCY		
❑ 7412	Land Rover - Alpes Martimes	£13-17
❑ 7415	Land Rover - Des Ardennes	£13-17
❑ 55602	Diamond T980 crane	£42
❑ 70501	Renault 1000KG - Bray en Val	£13-17
❑ 70505	Renault 1000KG - Magnac Bourg	£13-17
❑ 70601	Peugeot D3A - Pyrennes Atlantiques	£13-17
❑ 70605	Peugeot D3A - Rombach le Franc	£13-17
❑ 70901	Saviem escape ladder	£30-35
❑ 71203	Renault water tanker	£30-35
❑ 73501	Berliet escape ladder	£30-35
❑ 73502	Berliet escape ladder - Marseille	£30-35
❑ 73603	Berliet GLR - Var	£30-35
❑ 74401	Citroen Type 55 escape ladder	£30-35
❑ 74402	Citroen Type 55 - Electro Ventilateur	£30-35
❑ 74403	Citroen Type 55 escape ladder	£30-35
❑ EX02401	VW minibus - Cruseilles fire	£13-17

Pair of ERF & Albion Corgi CAFÉ Connection sets. Sold for £50 DJ Auctions

Ref.	Model	Price Guide
❑ EX07402	Land Rover - Marseilles Fire	£13-17
❑ EX07717	Land Rover - Bouche de Rhone	£13-17
❑ EX30521	Renault 1000kg military ambulance	£13-17
❑ EX51706	Dodge - Beziers Fire	£13-17
❑ EX70208	Berliet GLR Turntable ladder - Ville de Avignon	£21
❑ EX70519	Renault 1000KG - Gendarmerie	£13-17
❑ EX70521	Renault 1000KG military ambulance	£13-17
❑ EX70522	Renault 1000KG - Paris Fire Brigade	£13-17
❑ EX70523	Renault 1000KG - Marseilles Ambulance	£13-17
❑ EX70526	Renault 1000KG - Limoges Fire Brigade	£13-17
❑ EX70534	Renault 1000KG - Sapeurs Pompiers de Blace	£13-17
❑ EX70538	Renault 1000KG ambulance - Pompiers d'Oise	£13-17
❑ EX70618	Peugeot D3A - Police	£13-17
❑ EX70619	Peugeot D3A - Ambulance	£13-17
❑ EX70627	Peugeot D3A - Pompiers d'Ouroux ambulance	£13-17
❑ EX70909	Saviem JL20 turntable ladder - Paris	£23
❑ EX72014	Bernard - St Raphael Quinquina	£13-17
❑ EX72916	UNIC Saverne - Pompes Guinard	£13-17
❑ EX74004	Ciroen 55 turntable ladder - Paris	£21

MILITARY

Ref.	Model	Price Guide
❑ 55102	Diamond T Tank Transporter & Tank	£33
❑ 73801	Berliet GLR8	£35
❑ 74001	Citroen Type 55	£33

A pair of unboxed Harris & Minors commercials.
Sold for £21 Toy Price Guide Archive

Eddie Stobart remote control set, made in 2003.
Sold for £19 Toy price Guide Archive

J8/1 Simon Snorkel Fire Engine released in 1990.
Sold for 99p Toy Price Guide Archive

Chevrolet Bel Air 1:43 scale in blue/white

19302 Bedford S lorry in Weetabix livery,
10000 Limited edition issued in 1996.
Sold for £14 Toy Price Guide Archive

J12 Iveco Petrol Tanker released in 1984 for mass
sale through supermarket retail outlets.

CC12502 Eddie Stobart Atkinson Flatbed

CC13207 Eddie Stobart DAF. Sold unboxed for £17
Toy Price Guide Archive

AA34501 The Wright Flyer, scarcer version
on launching ramp

AA34503 The Wright Flyer

Creative use of the promotional literature in the
form of this 45 inch single for the Beatle Collection
issued in 1997. This example cost £3 from Ebay

96011 Mr Bean's Mini with figure